Tasty Slow Cooker Dishes

The Family Food Collection

D1644537

LOVE FOOD™

First published in 2012
LOVE FOOD is an imprint of Parragon Books Ltd

Parragon
Queen Street House
4 Queen Street
Bath BA1 1HE, UK

www.parragon.com

ISBN: 978-1-4454-7905-7

Printed in China

Produced by Ivy Contract
Cover and additional internal photography by Mike Cooper
Cover and additional home economy and food styling by Lincoln Jefferson
New recipes written by Christine France

Notes for the Reader

This book uses both metric and imperial measurements. Follow the same units of measurement throughout; do not mix metric and imperial. All spoon measurements are level: teaspoons are assumed to be 5 ml, and tablespoons are assumed to be 15 ml. Unless otherwise stated, milk is assumed to be full fat, eggs and individual vegetables are medium, and pepper is freshly ground black pepper.

The times given are an approximate guide only. Preparation times differ according to the techniques used by different people and the cooking times may also vary from those given. Optional ingredients, variations or serving suggestions have not been included in the calculations.

Recipes using raw or very lightly cooked eggs should be avoided by infants, the elderly, pregnant women, convalescents and anyone suffering from an illness. Pregnant and breastfeeding women are advised to avoid eating peanuts and peanut products. Sufferers from nut allergies should be aware that some of the ready-made ingredients used in the recipes in this book may contain nuts. Always check the packaging before use.

Vegetarians should be aware that some of the ready-made ingredients used in the recipes in this book may contain animal products. Always check the packaging before use.

Tasty Slow Cooker Dishes

introduction	4
to start	6
everyday	36
entertaining	88
around the world	140
desserts	184
index	208

introduction

For busy people, a slow cooker can provide that most elusive culinary combination: healthy home-cooked food *and* convenience. With minimum effort, you can serve up a meal that is tender and flavoursome whilst saving time and money – what could be better? Just put the ingredients into the slow cooker in the morning, switch it on and leave it to cook whilst you go to work and get on with your life. As the slow cooker cooks at a very low temperature, cooking times are quite flexible – you needn't worry about your meal burning if you are a little late, and even an amateur cook can rustle up a spectacular dish.

For the health conscious, slow cooking doesn't require much oil, and the nutrients in vegetables stay in the pot rather than being lost through boiling and draining. Slow cooking makes cheaper, tougher cuts of meat deliciously tender, saving you money on your shopping, and because a slow cooker only uses as much electricity as a lightbulb it will cut down your electricity bill too! All kinds of dishes can be prepared, and because everything is cooked in one pot there is less washing-up to do afterwards.

This book will introduce you to the range of sumptuous meals that you can prepare in your slow cooker, from warming winter casseroles, low-fat vegetable soups and spicy curries to indulgent desserts. There are dishes to suit every occasion and taste with a mouth-watering selection of meals that are suitable for all the family. All it needs is a little planning and preparation in advance so you can be assured that the perfect meal will be waiting for you when you return at the end of the day.

All the recipes featured in this book will fit into a 4.5 litre capacity slow cooker. Models vary slightly from one manufacturer to another, so make sure you check the instructions for your particular slow cooker, however the basics apply to all models. So turn the page, choose a recipe for a simple starter or a magnificent main course, and get ready to save money, eat healthily, and rediscover time just for you.

to start

chicken noodle soup

ingredients

serves 4

1 onion, diced
2 celery sticks, diced
2 carrots, diced
1 kg/2 lb 4 oz oven-ready chicken
700 ml/1¼ pints hot chicken stock
115 g/4 oz dried egg tagliatelle
2 tbsp chopped fresh dill, plus
    extra for serving
salt and pepper

method

1 Preheat the slow cooker, if necessary, or according to the manufacturer's instructions.

2 Place the onion, celery and carrots in the slow cooker. Season the chicken all over with salt and pepper and place on top. Pour the stock over. Cover and cook on low for 5 hours.

3 Carefully lift out the chicken and remove the meat from the carcass, discarding the bones and skin. Cut the meat into bite-sized pieces.

4 Skim the excess fat from the juices, then return the chicken to the slow cooker. Turn the setting to high.

5 Bring a large saucepan of lightly salted water to the boil. Add the tagliatelle, return to the boil and cook for 5 minutes. Drain well.

6 Stir the tagliatelle and dill into the pot, cover and cook on high for a further 20 minutes. Serve immediately, in wide bowls, sprinkled with dill.

new england clam chowder

ingredients

serves 4

25 g/1 oz butter
1 onion, finely chopped
2 potatoes, peeled and cut
    into cubes
1 large carrot, diced
400 ml/14 fl oz fish stock or water
280 g/10 oz canned clams, drained
250 ml/9 fl oz double cream
salt and pepper
chopped fresh parsley, to garnish
fresh crusty bread, to serve

method

1 Preheat the slow cooker, if necessary, or according to the manufacturer's instructions.

2 Melt the butter in a frying pan, add the onion and fry over a medium heat for 4–5 minutes, stirring, until the onion is golden.

3 Transfer the onion to the slow cooker with the potatoes, carrot, stock and salt and pepper. Cover and cook on high for 3 hours.

4 Add the clams and the cream to the slow cooker and stir to mix evenly. Cover and cook for a further 1 hour.

5 Adjust the seasoning to taste then sprinkle with parsley and serve with crusty bread.

tomato & lentil soup

ingredients

serves 4

2 tbsp sunflower oil
1 onion, chopped
1 garlic clove, finely chopped
2 celery sticks, chopped
2 carrots, chopped
1 tsp ground cumin
1 tsp ground coriander
175 g/6 oz red or yellow lentils
1 tbsp tomato purée
1.2 litres/2 pints vegetable stock
400 g/14 oz canned
    chopped tomatoes
1 bay leaf
salt and pepper
crème fraîche and toasted crusty
    bread, to serve

method

1 Preheat the slow cooker, if necessary, or according
   to the manufacturer's instructions.

2 Heat the oil in a saucepan. Add the onion and garlic
   and cook over a low heat, stirring occasionally, for
   5 minutes, until softened. Stir in the celery and carrots
   and cook, stirring occasionally, for a further 4 minutes.
   Stir in the ground cumin and coriander and cook,
   stirring, for 1 minute, then add the lentils.

3 Mix the tomato purée with a little of the stock in a
   small bowl and add to the pan with the remaining
   stock, the tomatoes and bay leaf. Bring to the boil,
   then transfer to the slow cooker. Stir well, cover and
   cook on low for 3$\frac{1}{2}$–4 hours.

4 Remove and discard the bay leaf. Transfer the soup
   to a food processor or blender and process until
   smooth. Season to taste with salt and pepper. Ladle
   into warmed soup bowls, top each with a swirl of
   crème fraîche and serve immediately with toasted
   crusty bread.

greek bean & vegetable soup

ingredients

serves 4-6

500 g/1 lb 2 oz dried haricot
beans, soaked in cold water
overnight
2 onions, finely chopped
2 garlic cloves, finely chopped
2 potatoes, chopped
2 carrots, chopped
2 tomatoes, peeled and chopped
2 celery sticks, chopped
4 tbsp extra virgin olive oil
1 bay leaf
salt and pepper
12 black olives, stoned and
halved and 2 tbsp chopped
fresh chives, to serve

method

1 Preheat the slow cooker, if necessary, or according
to the manufacturer's instructions.

2 Drain the beans and rinse well under cold running
water. Place them in the slow cooker and add the
onions, garlic, potatoes, carrots, tomatoes, celery, olive
oil and bay leaf.

3 Pour in 2 litres/3½ pints boiling water, making sure
that all the ingredients are fully submerged. Cover and
cook on low for 12 hours until the beans are tender.

4 Remove and discard the bay leaf. Season the soup to
taste with salt and pepper and stir in the olives and
chives. Ladle into warmed soup bowls or large mugs
and serve.

cock-a-leekie soup

ingredients

serves 6–8

12 prunes, stoned, or
    12 ready-to-eat prunes
4 chicken portions
450 g/1 lb leeks, sliced
1.4 litres/2½ pints hot chicken
    or beef stock
1 bouquet garni
salt and pepper

method

1 Preheat the slow cooker, if necessary, or according to the manufacturer's instructions.

2 If using ordinary prunes, place them in a bowl and add cold water to cover. Set aside to soak while the soup is cooking.

3 Place the chicken portions and leeks in the slow cooker. Pour in the stock and add the bouquet garni. Cover and cook on low for 7 hours.

4 If you are going to serve the chicken in the soup, remove it from the cooker with a slotted spoon and cut the meat off the bones. Cut it into bite-sized pieces and return it to the cooker. Otherwise, leave the chicken portions in the slow cooker.

5 Drain the prunes, if necessary. Add the prunes to the soup and season to taste with salt and pepper. Re-cover and cook on high for 30 minutes.

6 Remove and discard the bouquet garni. Either ladle the soup, including the cut-up chicken, into warmed bowls or remove the chicken portions and keep warm for the main course, then ladle the broth into warmed bowls. Serve immediately.

bacon & lentil soup

ingredients

serves 6

450 g/1 lb thick, rindless smoked
    bacon rashers, diced
1 onion, chopped
2 carrots, sliced
2 celery sticks, chopped
1 turnip, chopped
1 large potato, chopped
85 g/3 oz green lentils
1 bouquet garni
1 litre/1¾ pints chicken
    stock or water
salt and pepper

method

1 Preheat the slow cooker, if necessary, or according
    to the manufacturer's instructions.

2 Heat a large, heavy-based saucepan. Add the bacon
    and cook over a low heat, stirring frequently, for
    4–5 minutes, until the fat runs. Add the onion, carrots,
    celery, turnip and potato and cook, stirring frequently,
    for 5 minutes.

3 Add the lentils and bouquet garni and pour in the
    stock. Bring to the boil, then transfer the mixture to
    the slow cooker. Cover and cook on low for 8–9 hours,
    or until the lentils are tender.

4 Remove and discard the bouquet garni and season the
    soup to taste with pepper and salt, if necessary. Ladle
    into warmed soup bowls and serve.

tex-mex bean dip

ingredients

serves 6

2 tbsp sunflower oil
1 onion, finely chopped
2 garlic cloves, finely chopped
2–3 fresh green chillies,
    deseeded and finely chopped
400 g/14 oz canned refried beans
    or red kidney beans
2 tbsp chilli sauce or taco sauce
6 tbsp hot vegetable stock
115 g/4 oz grated Cheddar cheese
salt and pepper
1 fresh red chilli, deseeded and
    shredded, to garnish
tortilla chips, to serve

method

1 Preheat the slow cooker, if necessary, or according
   to the manufacturer's instructions.

2 Heat the oil in a large, heavy-based frying pan. Add the
   onion, garlic and chillies and cook, stirring occasionally,
   over a low heat for 5 minutes until the onion is soft and
   translucent. Transfer to the slow cooker.

3 Add the refried beans to the slow cooker. If using red
   kidney beans, drain well and rinse under cold running
   water. Reserve 2 tablespoons of the beans and mash
   the remainder coarsely with a potato masher. Add all
   the beans to the slow cooker.

4 Add the sauce, hot stock and grated cheese, season
   with salt and pepper and stir well. Cover and cook on
   low for 2 hours.

5 Transfer the dip to a serving bowl, garnish with
   shredded red chilli and serve warm with tortilla chips
   on the side.

sweet & sour chicken wings

ingredients

serves 4

1 kg/2 lb 4 oz chicken wings,
    tips removed
2 celery sticks, chopped
700 ml/1¼ pints hot
    chicken stock
2 tbsp cornflour
3 tbsp white wine vinegar
    or rice vinegar
3 tbsp dark soy sauce
5 tbsp sweet chilli sauce
55 g/2 oz brown sugar
400 g/14 oz canned pineapple
    chunks in juice, drained
200 g/7 oz canned sliced bamboo
    shoots, drained and rinsed
½ yellow pepper, deseeded and
    thinly sliced
½ red pepper, deseeded and
    thinly sliced
salt

method

1 Preheat the slow cooker, if necessary, or according
   to the manufacturer's instructions.

2 Put the chicken wings and celery in the slow cooker
   and season with salt. Pour in the chicken stock, cover
   and cook on low for 5 hours.

3 Drain the chicken wings, reserving 350 ml/12 fl oz of
   the stock, and keep warm. Pour the reserved stock into
   a saucepan and stir in the cornflour. Add the vinegar,
   soy sauce and chilli sauce. Place over a medium heat
   and stir in the sugar. Cook, stirring constantly, for
   5 minutes, or until the sugar has dissolved completely
   and the sauce is thickened, smooth and clear.

4 Lower the heat, stir in the pineapple, bamboo shoots
   and peppers and simmer gently for 2–3 minutes. Stir
   in the chicken wings until they are thoroughly coated,
   then transfer to serving bowls.

warm chickpea salad

ingredients

serves 4

225 g/8 oz dried chickpeas,
    soaked overnight in cold
    water and drained
115 g/4 oz stoned black olives
4 spring onions, finely chopped
fresh parsley sprigs, to garnish
crusty bread, to serve

dressing

2 tbsp red wine vinegar
2 tbsp mixed chopped fresh herbs,
    such as parsley, rosemary
    and thyme
3 garlic cloves, very finely chopped
125 ml/4 fl oz extra virgin olive oil
salt and pepper

method

1 Preheat the slow cooker, if necessary, or according
   to the manufacturer's instructions.

2 Place the chickpeas in the slow cooker and add
   sufficient boiling water to cover. Cover and cook
   on low for 12 hours.

3 Drain well and transfer to a bowl. Stir in the olives
   and spring onions.

4 To make the dressing, whisk together the vinegar,
   herbs and garlic in a jug and season with salt and
   pepper to taste. Gradually whisk in the olive oil. Pour
   the dressing over the still-warm chickpeas and toss
   lightly to coat. Garnish with the parsley sprigs and
   serve warm with crusty bread.

boston baked beans

ingredients

serves 4–6

450 g/1 lb dried white haricot
beans, soaked overnight in cold
water and drained
115 g/4 oz salt pork, soaked in
cold water for 3 hours
and drained
3 tbsp black treacle
3 tbsp muscovado sugar
2 tsp dry mustard
1 onion, chopped
salt and pepper

method

1 Preheat the slow cooker, if necessary, or according
to the manufacturer's instructions.

2 Place the beans in the slow cooker and add about
1.4 litres/2½ pints boiling water so that they are
covered. Cover and cook the beans on high for 3 hours.
Meanwhile, cut the salt pork into chunks.

3 Drain the beans, reserving 225 ml/8 fl oz of the cooking
liquid. Mix the reserved liquid with the treacle, sugar,
mustard and 1 teaspoon salt.

4 Return the beans to the slow cooker and add the salt
pork, onion and the treacle mixture. Stir, then cover
and cook on low for 11 hours. Adjust the seasoning
and serve immediately.

louisiana courgettes

ingredients

serves 6

1 kg/2 lb 4 oz courgettes,
    thickly sliced
1 onion, finely chopped
2 garlic cloves, finely chopped
2 red peppers, deseeded and
    chopped
5 tbsp hot vegetable stock
4 tomatoes, peeled and chopped
25 g/1 oz butter, diced
salt and cayenne pepper

method

1 Preheat the slow cooker, if necessary, or according
   to the manufacturer's instructions.

2 Place the courgettes, onion, garlic and red peppers
   in the slow cooker and season to taste with salt and
   cayenne pepper. Pour in the stock and mix well.

3 Sprinkle the chopped tomatoes on top and dot with
   the butter. Cover and cook on high for 2½ hours
   until tender.

aubergine timbales

ingredients

serves 4

3 tbsp olive oil, plus extra
for greasing
2 onions, finely chopped
2 aubergines, halved with flesh
removed and shells reserved
2 red peppers, deseeded
and chopped
1 large tomato, peeled
and chopped
6 tbsp milk
2 egg yolks
pinch of ground cinnamon
85 g/3 oz crispbread, finely
crushed
salt and pepper
sprigs of fresh coriander, to garnish

sauce

300 ml/10 fl oz soured cream
3–4 tbsp sun-dried tomato purée
(optional)

method

1 Preheat the slow cooker, if necessary, or according
to the manufacturer's instructions.

2 Heat the oil in a large, heavy-based frying pan. Add the
onions and cook over a low heat for 5 minutes. Add
the aubergine flesh, peppers and tomato and cook for
15–20 minutes, until all the vegetables are soft. Transfer
the mixture to a food processor or blender and process
to a purée, then scrape into a bowl. Beat together the
milk, egg yolks, cinnamon and salt and pepper in a jug,
then stir into the vegetable purée.

3 Brush 4 ramekins or cups with oil and sprinkle with the
crispbread crumbs to coat. Mix about three-quarters
of the remaining crumbs into the vegetable purée.
Slice the aubergine shells into strips and use them to
line the ramekins. Spoon the filling into the ramekins,
and fold the overlapping strips over the top.

4 Cover with foil and place in the slow cooker. Pour in
boiling water to one-third of the way up the sides of
the ramekins. Cover and cook on high for 2 hours.

5 To make the sauce, lightly beat the soured cream and
add the tomato purée to taste, if using. Season with
salt and pepper. Lift the ramekins out of the cooker
and remove the foil. Invert onto serving plates and
serve with the sauce, garnished with coriander sprigs.

cabbage roulades with tomato sauce

ingredients

serves 4

225 g/8 oz mixed nuts,
    finely ground
2 onions, finely chopped
2 garlic cloves, finely chopped
2 celery sticks, finely chopped
115 g/4 oz grated Cheddar cheese
1 tsp finely chopped thyme
2 eggs
1 tsp yeast extract
12 large green cabbage leaves

tomato sauce

2 tbsp sunflower oil
2 onions, chopped
2 garlic cloves, finely chopped
600 g/1 lb 5 oz canned
    chopped tomatoes
2 tbsp tomato purée
1½ tsp sugar
salt and pepper

method

1 Preheat the slow cooker, if necessary, or according
   to the manufacturer's instructions.

2 First make the tomato sauce. Heat the oil in a saucepan.
   Add the onions and cook over a medium heat, stirring
   occasionally, for 5 minutes until softened. Stir in the
   garlic and cook for 1 minute, then add the tomatoes,
   tomato purée and sugar. Season with salt and pepper
   and bring to the boil. Lower the heat and simmer
   gently for 20 minutes until thickened.

3 Meanwhile, mix together the nuts, onions, garlic, celery,
   cheese and thyme in a bowl. Lightly beat the eggs with
   the yeast extract in a jug, then stir into the nut mixture.

4 Cut out the thick stalks from the cabbage leaves.
   Blanch the leaves in a large saucepan of boiling water
   for 5 minutes, then drain and refresh under cold water.
   Pat dry with kitchen paper. Place a little of the nut
   mixture on the stalk end of each cabbage leaf. Fold
   the sides over, then roll up to make a neat parcel.

5 Arrange the parcels in the slow cooker, seam side
   down. Pour the sauce over the cabbage parcels. Cover
   and cook on low for 3–4 hours. Serve the cabbage
   roulades hot or cold.

everyday

parmesan chicken

ingredients

serves 4

1 egg, beaten
4 skinless, boneless chicken breasts
85 g/3 oz fine dry breadcrumbs
2 tbsp olive oil
350 g/12 oz ready-made
    tomato-based pasta sauce
4 thin slices Cheddar cheese
115 g/4 oz finely grated Parmesan
    cheese
salt and pepper
cooked rice, to serve

method

1 Preheat the slow cooker, if necessary, or according to the manufacturer's instructions.

2 Season the egg with salt and pepper. Dip each chicken breast in the egg, turning to coat evenly, then dip into the breadcrumbs, lightly pressing down to cover evenly.

3 Heat the oil in a frying pan over a high heat, add the chicken breasts and fry quickly for 3–4 minutes, until golden brown, turning once.

4 Pour the pasta sauce into the slow cooker and place the chicken breasts on top. Cover and cook on low for 4 hours.

5 Place a slice of Cheddar cheese on top of each chicken breast and sprinkle with Parmesan cheese. Cover and cook on high for a further 20 minutes. Serve immediately with rice.

chicken & dumplings

ingredients

serves 4

2 tbsp olive oil
1 large onion, thinly sliced
2 carrots, cut into 2-cm/¾-inch
    chunks
225 g/8 oz French beans,
    cut into 2.5-cm/1-inch lengths
4 skinless, boneless chicken breasts
300 ml/10 fl oz hot chicken stock
salt and pepper

dumplings

200 g/7 oz self-raising flour
100 g/3½ oz shredded suet
4 tbsp chopped fresh parsley

method.

1 Preheat the slow cooker, if necessary, or according
   to the manufacturer's instructions.

2 Heat 1 tablespoon of oil in a frying pan, add the
   onion and fry over a high heat for 3–4 minutes, or
   until golden. Place in the slow cooker with the carrots
   and beans.

3 Add the remaining oil to the pan, then add the chicken
   breasts and fry until golden, turning once. Arrange on
   top of the vegetables in a single layer, season well with
   salt and pepper and pour over the stock. Cover and
   cook on low for 4 hours.

4 Turn the slow cooker up to high while making the
   dumplings. Sift the flour into a bowl and stir in the suet
   and parsley. Season to taste with salt and pepper. Stir
   in just enough cold water to make a fairly firm dough,
   mixing lightly. Divide into 12 and shape into small balls.

5 Arrange the dumplings on top of the chicken, cover
   and cook for 30 minutes on high. Serve immediately.

chicken & sweetcorn stew

ingredients

serves 4

3 tbsp sunflower oil
1 large onion, thinly sliced
1 green pepper, deseeded
    and chopped
8 chicken pieces, such as thighs
    and drumsticks
400 g/14 oz canned chopped
    tomatoes, drained
pinch of cayenne pepper
1 tbsp Worcestershire sauce
300 ml/10 fl oz hot chicken stock
1 tbsp cornflour
200 g/7 oz frozen sweetcorn,
    thawed
450 g/1 lb frozen broad beans,
    thawed
salt
crusty bread, to serve

method

1 Preheat the slow cooker, if necessary, or according
to the manufacturer's instructions.

2 Heat the oil in a large, heavy-based frying pan. Add
the onion and green pepper and cook over a medium
heat, stirring occasionally, for 5 minutes until the onion
is softened. Using a slotted spoon, transfer the mixture
to the slow cooker.

3 Add the chicken to the pan and cook, turning
occasionally, for 5 minutes until golden all over. Transfer
to the slow cooker and add the tomatoes. Season with
cayenne pepper and salt. Stir the Worcestershire sauce
into the hot stock and pour into the slow cooker. Cover
and cook on low for 6½ hours.

4 Mix the cornflour to a paste with 2–3 tablespoons
water and stir into the stew. Add the sweetcorn and
beans, re-cover and cook on high for 30–40 minutes
until everything is cooked through and piping hot.
Transfer the stew to warmed bowls and serve with
crusty bread.

chicken braised with red cabbage

ingredients

serves 4

2 tbsp sunflower oil
4 skinless chicken thighs
    or drumsticks
1 onion, chopped
500 g/1 lb 2 oz red cabbage,
    cored and shredded
2 apples, peeled and chopped
12 canned or cooked chestnuts,
    halved (optional)
½ tsp juniper berries
125 ml/4 fl oz red wine
salt and pepper
fresh flat-leaf parsley, to garnish

method

1 Preheat the slow cooker, if necessary, or according to the manufacturer's instructions.

2 Heat the oil in a large, heavy-based saucepan. Add the chicken and cook, turning frequently, for 5 minutes until golden on all sides. Using a slotted spoon, transfer to a plate lined with kitchen paper.

3 Add the onion to the saucepan and cook over a medium heat, stirring occasionally, until softened. Stir in the cabbage and apples and cook, stirring occasionally, for 5 minutes. Add the chestnuts, if using, juniper berries and wine and season to taste with salt and pepper. Bring to the boil.

4 Spoon half the cabbage mixture into the slow cooker, add the chicken pieces, then top with the remaining cabbage mixture. Cover and cook on low for 5 hours until the chicken is tender and cooked through. Serve immediately, garnished with the parsley.

chicken & apple pot

ingredients

serves 4

1 tbsp olive oil
4 chicken portions, about
    175 g/6 oz each
1 onion, chopped
2 celery sticks, coarsely chopped
1½ tbsp plain flour
300 ml/10 fl oz clear apple juice
150 ml/5 fl oz chicken stock
1 cooking apple, cored and
    cut into quarters
2 bay leaves
1–2 tsp clear honey
1 yellow pepper, deseeded
    and cut into chunks
salt and pepper

garnish

1 large or 2 medium eating apples,
    cored and sliced
1 tbsp butter, melted
2 tbsp demerara sugar
1 tbsp chopped fresh mint

method

1 Preheat the slow cooker, if necessary, or according
   to the manufacturer's instructions.

2 Heat the oil in a heavy-based frying pan. Add the
   chicken and cook over a medium–high heat, for
   10 minutes, until golden brown all over. Using a
   slotted spoon, transfer the chicken to the slow cooker.

3 Add the onion and celery to the pan and cook over
   a low heat, stirring occasionally, for 5 minutes, until
   softened. Sprinkle in the flour and cook, stirring
   constantly, for 2 minutes, then remove the pan from
   the heat. Stir in the apple juice and stock, then return
   the pan to the heat and bring to the boil, stirring
   constantly. Stir in the apple, bay leaves and honey
   and season to taste with salt and pepper.

4 Pour the mixture over the chicken, cover the slow
   cooker and cook on low for 6½ hours, until the chicken
   is tender and the juices run clear when the thickest
   part is pierced with a sharp knife. Stir in the yellow
   pepper, re-cover and cook on high for 45 minutes.

5 Preheat the grill. Brush the apple slices with the melted
   butter and sprinkle them with sugar. Grill for 2 minutes
   on each side until the sugar has caramelized. Serve the
   stew garnished with the caramelized apple slices and
   the mint.

turkey hash

ingredients

serves 4

1 tbsp olive oil
500 g/1 lb 2 oz turkey mince
1 large red onion, diced
550 g/1 lb 4 oz butternut
    squash, diced
2 celery sticks, sliced
500 g/1 lb 2 oz potatoes,
    peeled and diced
3 tbsp Worcestershire sauce
2 bay leaves
salt and pepper

method

1 Preheat the slow cooker, if necessary, or according to the manufacturer's instructions.

2 Heat the oil in a frying pan, add the turkey and fry over a high heat, stirring, until broken up and lightly browned all over.

3 Place all the vegetables in the slow cooker then add the turkey and pan juices. Add the Worcestershire sauce and bay leaves and season with salt and pepper. Cover and cook on low for 7 hours. Serve immediately.

turkey & rice casserole

ingredients

serves 4

1 tbsp olive oil
500 g/1 lb 2 oz diced
    turkey breast
1 onion, diced
2 carrots, diced
2 celery sticks, sliced
250 g/9 oz closed-cup
    mushrooms, sliced
175 g/6 oz long-grain rice,
    preferably Basmati
450 ml/16 fl oz hot chicken stock
salt and pepper

method

1 Preheat the slow cooker, if necessary, or according
   to the manufacturer's instructions.

2 Heat the oil in a heavy-based frying pan, add the
   turkey and fry over a high heat for 3–4 minutes, until
   lightly browned.

3 Combine the onion, carrots, celery, mushrooms and
   rice in the slow cooker. Arrange the turkey on top,
   season well with salt and pepper and pour the stock
   over. Cover and cook on high for 2 hours.

4 Stir lightly with a fork to mix, adjust the seasoning
   to taste and serve immediately.

pesto turkey pasta bake

ingredients

serves 4

250 g/9 oz dried macaroni
175 ml/6 fl oz tomato juice
500 g/1 lb 2 oz turkey mince
1 small onion, finely chopped
40 g/1½ oz fresh white
    breadcrumbs
100 g/3½ oz pesto sauce
125 g/4½ oz mozzarella cheese
salt and pepper
fresh basil leaves, to garnish

method

1 Preheat the slow cooker, if necessary, or according to the manufacturer's instructions.

2 Bring a large saucepan of lightly salted water to the boil, add the pasta, return to the boil and cook for half the amount of time stated on the pack (5–6 minutes). Drain well, place in the slow cooker and stir in the tomato juice.

3 Mix the turkey, onion and breadcrumbs together. Season well with salt and pepper. Divide the mixture into about 20 small balls, rolling them with your hands.

4 Arrange the meatballs over the pasta in a single layer and spoon a little of the pesto sauce on top of each. Cover and cook on high for 2 hours.

5 Tear the mozzarella cheese into small pieces and scatter over the meatballs. Cover and cook on high for a further 20 minutes. Serve immediately, garnished with fresh basil.

pot roast with beer

ingredients

serves 4-6

2 small onions, each cut
     into 8 wedges
8 small carrots, halved
     lengthways
1 fennel bulb, cut into 8 wedges
2.25 kg/5 lb rolled chuck steak
2 tbsp Dijon mustard
1 tbsp plain flour
100 ml/3½ fl oz beer
salt and pepper

method

1 Preheat the slow cooker, if necessary, or according
   to the manufacturer's instructions.

2 Place the onions, carrots and fennel in the slow cooker
   and season to taste with salt and pepper. Place the
   beef on top.

3 Mix the mustard and flour together to form a paste
   and spread over the beef. Season well and pour over
   the beer. Cover and cook on low for 8 hours.

4 Carefully remove the beef and vegetables and place
   on a warmed platter. Skim the excess fat from the
   juices and pour into a jug to serve with the beef.

spicy beef

ingredients

serves 4

1½ tbsp plain flour
450 g/1 lb stewing steak,
    cut into 2.5-cm/1-inch cubes
2 tbsp olive oil
1 Spanish onion, chopped
3–4 garlic cloves, crushed
1 green chilli, deseeded
    and chopped
3 celery sticks, sliced
4 cloves
1 tsp ground allspice
1–2 tsp hot pepper sauce
600 ml/1 pint beef stock
225 g/8 oz peeled acorn or other
    squash, cut into small chunks
1 large red pepper, deseeded
    and chopped
4 tomatoes, coarsely chopped
115 g/4 oz okra, trimmed
    and halved
mixed wild and long-grain rice,
    to serve

method

1 Preheat the slow cooker, if necessary, or according
   to the manufacturer's instructions.

2 Spread out the flour in a shallow dish, add the steak
   cubes and toss until well coated. Shake off any excess
   and reserve the remaining flour.

3 Heat the oil in a heavy-based frying pan. Add the
   onion, garlic, chilli, celery, cloves and allspice and
   cook over a low heat, stirring occasionally, for
   5 minutes until the vegetables have softened.
   Increase the heat to high, add the steak cubes and
   cook, stirring frequently, for 3 minutes until browned
   all over. Sprinkle in the reserved flour and cook, stirring
   constantly, for 2 minutes, then remove the pan from
   the heat.

4 Stir in the hot pepper sauce, then gradually stir in the
   stock. Return the pan to the heat and bring to the boil,
   stirring constantly. Transfer the mixture to the slow
   cooker and add the squash. Cover and cook on low
   for 8 hours.

5 Add the red pepper, tomatoes and okra, re-cover and
   cook on high for 1 hour. Serve with mixed wild and
   long-grain rice.

beef & button onions

ingredients

serves 4-6

2 tbsp olive oil
450 g/1 lb button onions,
     peeled but left whole
2 garlic cloves, halved
900 g/2 lb stewing beef, cubed
½ tsp ground cinnamon
1 tsp ground cloves
1 tsp ground cumin
2 tbsp tomato purée
75 cl bottle red wine
grated rind and juice of 1 orange
1 bay leaf
salt and pepper
1 tbsp chopped fresh flat-leaf
     parsley, to garnish
boiled new potatoes, to serve

method

1 Preheat the slow cooker, if necessary, or according to the manufacturer's instructions.

2 Heat the oil in a heavy-based frying pan. Add the onions and garlic and cook over a medium heat, stirring frequently, for 5 minutes until softened and beginning to brown. Increase the heat to high, add the beef and cook, stirring frequently, for 5 minutes, until browned all over.

3 Stir in the cinnamon, cloves, cumin and tomato purée and season with salt and pepper. Pour in the wine, scraping up any sediment from the base of the frying pan. Stir in the orange rind and juice, add the bay leaf and bring to the boil.

4 Transfer the mixture to the slow cooker, cover and cook on low for 9 hours, until the beef is tender. If possible, stir the stew once during the second half of the cooking time.

5 Serve the stew garnished with the parsley and accompanied by boiled new potatoes.

provençal beef & olives

ingredients

serves 4-6

900 g/2 lb stewing steak, cubed
2 onions, thinly sliced
2 carrots, sliced
4 large garlic cloves, lightly
    crushed
1 bouquet garni
4 juniper berries
500 ml/18 fl oz dry red wine
2 tbsp brandy
2 tbsp olive oil
3 tbsp plain flour
175 g/6 oz lardons or diced bacon
2 x 10-cm/4-inch strips of thinly
    pared orange rind
85 g/3 oz stoned black olives,
    rinsed
salt and pepper
1 tbsp chopped fresh flat-leaf
    parsley and 1 tbsp finely grated
    orange rind, to garnish
tagliatelle or buttered noodles,
    to serve

method

1 Preheat the slow cooker, if necessary, or according
   to the manufacturer's instructions.

2 Put the stewing steak in a large, non-metallic dish. Add
   the onions, carrots, garlic, bouquet garni and juniper
   berries and season with salt and pepper. Combine the
   wine, brandy and olive oil in a jug and pour the mixture
   over the meat and vegetables. Cover with clingfilm
   and marinate in the refrigerator for 24 hours.

3 Using a slotted spoon, remove the steak from the
   marinade and pat dry with kitchen paper. Reserve
   the marinade, vegetables and flavourings. Place the
   flour in a shallow dish and season well with salt and
   pepper. Toss the steak cubes in the flour until well
   coated and shake off any excess.

4 Sprinkle half the lardons in the base of the slow cooker
   and top with the steak cubes. Pour in the marinade,
   including the vegetables and flavourings, and add
   the strips of orange rind and the olives. Top with the
   remaining lardons. Cover and cook on low for 9½–10
   hours, until the steak and vegetables are tender.

5 Remove and discard the bouquet garni and skim
   off any fat that has risen to the surface of the stew.
   Sprinkle the parsley and grated orange rind over the
   top and serve with tagliatelle or buttered noodles.

goulash

ingredients

serves 4

4 tbsp sunflower oil
650 g/1 lb 7 oz braising steak,
    cut into 2.5-cm/1-inch cubes
2 tsp plain flour
2 tsp paprika
300 ml/10 fl oz beef stock
3 onions, chopped
4 carrots, diced
1 large potato or 2 medium
    potatoes, diced
1 bay leaf
$^1/_2$–1 tsp caraway seeds
400 g/14 oz canned
    chopped tomatoes
2 tbsp soured cream
salt and pepper

method

1 Preheat the slow cooker, if necessary, or according
    to the manufacturer's instructions.

2 Heat half the oil in a heavy-based frying pan. Add the
    beef and cook over a medium heat, stirring frequently,
    until browned all over. Lower the heat and stir in the
    flour and paprika. Cook, stirring constantly, for
    2 minutes. Gradually stir in the stock and bring to the
    boil, then transfer the mixture to the slow cooker.

3 Rinse out the frying pan and heat the remaining oil in
    it. Add the onions and cook over a low heat, stirring
    occasionally, for 5 minutes until softened. Stir in the
    carrots and potato and cook for a few minutes more.
    Add the bay leaf, caraway seeds and tomatoes with
    their can juices. Season with salt and pepper.

4 Transfer the vegetable mixture to the slow cooker, stir
    well, then cover and cook on low for 9 hours until the
    meat is tender.

5 Remove and discard the bay leaf. Pour over the soured
    cream and serve immediately.

variation

For a slightly sweeter spice, substitute 1 teaspoon of
paprika for sweet paprika and add 1 teaspoon of sugar.

lamb with red peppers

ingredients

serves 4

1½ tbsp plain flour
1 tsp ground cloves
450 g/1 lb boneless lamb,
    cut into thin strips
1–1½ tbsp olive oil
1 white onion, sliced
2–3 garlic cloves, sliced
300 ml/10 fl oz orange juice
150 ml/5 fl oz lamb or
    chicken stock
1 cinnamon stick
2 red peppers, deseeded and
    sliced into rings
4 tomatoes
4 fresh coriander sprigs
salt and pepper
1 tbsp chopped fresh coriander,
    to garnish
mashed sweet potatoes mixed
    with chopped spring onions
    and green beans, to serve

method

1 Preheat the slow cooker, if necessary, or according
   to the manufacturer's instructions.

2 Combine the flour and ground cloves in a shallow dish,
   add the strips of lamb and toss well to coat, shaking off
   any excess. Reserve the remaining spiced flour.

3 Heat 1 tablespoon of the oil in a heavy-based frying
   pan, add the lamb and cook over a high heat, stirring
   frequently, for 3 minutes, until browned all over. Using
   a slotted spoon, transfer the lamb to the slow cooker.
   Add the onion and garlic to the frying pan, with the
   remaining oil if necessary, and cook over a low heat,
   stirring occasionally, for 5 minutes, until softened.
   Sprinkle in the reserved spiced flour and cook, stirring
   constantly, for 2 minutes, then remove the pan from the
   heat. Stir in the orange juice and stock, then return the
   pan to the heat and bring to the boil, stirring constantly.

4 Pour the mixture over the lamb, add the cinnamon
   stick, red peppers, tomatoes and coriander sprigs and
   stir well. Cover and cook on low for 7–8 hours until the
   meat is tender. Remove and discard the cinnamon
   stick and coriander sprigs. Season to taste with salt and
   pepper, sprinkle the stew with chopped coriander and
   serve with mashed sweet potatoes with spring onions
   and green beans.

ham with black-eyed beans

ingredients

serves 4

2–3 tbsp olive oil
550 g/1 lb 4 oz lean gammon,
    trimmed and cut into
    4-cm/1½-inch pieces
1 onion, chopped
2–3 garlic cloves, chopped
2 celery sticks, chopped
175 g/6 oz carrots, thinly sliced
1 cinnamon stick
½ tsp ground cloves
¼ tsp freshly grated nutmeg
1 tsp dried oregano
450 ml/16 fl oz chicken or
    vegetable stock
2 tbsp maple syrup
225 g/8 oz chorizo or other spicy
    sausages, skinned
400 g/14 oz canned black-eyed
    beans, drained and rinsed
1 orange pepper, deseeded and
    chopped
1 tbsp cornflour
pepper
sprig of fresh flat-leaf parsley or
    oregano, to garnish

method

1 Preheat the slow cooker, if necessary, or according
   to the manufacturer's instructions.

2 Heat 1 tablespoon of the oil in a heavy-based frying
   pan, add the gammon and cook over a high heat,
   stirring frequently, for 5 minutes until browned all over.
   Using a slotted spoon, transfer to the slow cooker.

3 Add 1 tablespoon of the remaining oil to the frying
   pan. Reduce the heat to low, add the onion, garlic,
   celery and carrots and cook, stirring occasionally, for
   5 minutes until softened. Add the cinnamon, cloves
   and nutmeg, season with pepper and cook, stirring
   constantly, for 2 minutes. Stir in the dried oregano,
   stock and maple syrup and bring to the boil, stirring
   constantly. Pour the mixture over the gammon, stir
   well, cover and cook on low for 5–6 hours.

4 Heat the remaining oil in a frying pan, add the chorizo
   and cook for 10 minutes, until browned all over.
   Remove from the pan, cut each into 3–4 chunks and
   add to the slow cooker with the black-eyed beans and
   orange pepper. Re-cover and cook on high for 1–1½
   hours. Stir the cornflour with 2 tablespoons water to a
   smooth paste in a bowl, then stir into the stew, re-cover
   and cook on high for 15 minutes. Discard the cinnamon
   stick, garnish the stew with a fresh herb sprig and serve.

tagliatelle with prawns

ingredients

serves 4

400 g/14 oz tomatoes,
    peeled and chopped
140 g/5 oz tomato purée
1 garlic clove, finely chopped
2 tbsp chopped fresh parsley
500 g/1 lb 2 oz cooked, peeled
    Mediterranean prawns
6 fresh basil leaves, torn
400 g/14 oz dried tagliatelle
salt and pepper
fresh basil leaves, to garnish

method

1 Preheat the slow cooker, if necessary, or according to the manufacturer's instructions.

2 Put the tomatoes, tomato purée, garlic and parsley in the slow cooker and season with salt and pepper. Cover and cook on low for 7 hours.

3 Add the prawns and basil. Re-cover and cook on high for 15 minutes.

4 Meanwhile, bring a large saucepan of lightly salted water to the boil. Add the pasta, bring back to the boil and cook for 10–12 minutes until tender but still firm to the bite.

5 Drain the pasta and tip it into a warmed serving bowl. Add the prawn sauce and toss lightly with 2 large forks. Garnish with the basil leaves and serve immediately.

spiced seafood & okra

ingredients

serves 6

2 tbsp sunflower oil
175 g/6 oz okra, trimmed and
    cut into 2.5-cm/1-inch pieces
2 onions, finely chopped
4 celery sticks, very finely chopped
1 garlic clove, finely chopped
2 tbsp plain flour
½ tsp sugar
1 tsp ground cumin
700 ml/1¼ pints fish stock
1 red pepper, deseeded and
    chopped
1 green pepper, deseeded
    and chopped
2 large tomatoes, chopped
4 tbsp chopped fresh parsley
1 tbsp chopped fresh coriander
dash of Tabasco
350 g/12 oz large raw prawns,
    peeled and deveined
350 g/12 oz cod or haddock fillets,
    skinned and cut into 2.5-cm/
    1-inch chunks
350 g/12 oz monkfish fillet,
    cut into 2.5-cm/1-inch chunks
salt and pepper

method

1 Preheat the slow cooker, if necessary, or according
to the manufacturer's instructions.

2 Heat half the oil in a heavy-based frying pan. Add the
okra and cook over a low heat, stirring frequently, for
5 minutes until browned. Using a slotted spoon,
transfer the okra to the slow cooker.

3 Add the remaining oil to the frying pan. Add the
onions and celery and cook over a low heat, stirring
occasionally, for 5 minutes until softened. Add the
garlic and cook, stirring frequently, for 1 minute, then
sprinkle in the flour, sugar and cumin and season with
salt and pepper. Cook, stirring constantly, for 2 minutes,
then remove the frying pan from the heat.

4 Gradually stir in the stock, then return the pan to the
heat and bring to the boil, stirring constantly. Pour
the mixture over the okra and stir in the peppers and
tomatoes. Cover and cook on low for 5–6 hours.

5 Stir in the parsley, coriander and Tabasco to taste, then
add the prawns, cod and monkfish. Cover and cook
on high for 30 minutes until the fish and prawns are
ready. Taste and adjust the seasoning if necessary
and serve.

south-western seafood

ingredients

serves 4

2 tbsp olive oil, plus extra
    for drizzling
1 large onion, chopped
4 garlic cloves, finely chopped
1 yellow pepper, deseeded
    and chopped
1 red pepper, deseeded
    and chopped
1 orange pepper, deseeded
    and chopped
450 g/1 lb tomatoes,
    peeled and chopped
2 large, mild green chillies,
    such as poblano, chopped
finely grated rind and
    juice of 1 lime
2 tbsp chopped fresh coriander,
    plus extra leaves to garnish
1 bay leaf
450 ml/16 fl oz fish, vegetable
    or chicken stock
450 g/1 lb red mullet fillets
450 g/1 lb raw prawns
225 g/8 oz prepared squid
salt and pepper

method

1 Preheat the slow cooker, if necessary, or according
    to the manufacturer's instructions.

2 Heat the oil in a saucepan. Add the onion and garlic
    and cook over a low heat, stirring occasionally, for
    5 minutes until softened. Add the peppers, tomatoes
    and chillies and cook, stirring frequently, for 5 minutes.
    Stir in the lime rind and juice, add the coriander and
    bay leaf and pour in the stock. Bring the mixture to
    a boil, stirring occasionally.

3 Transfer the mixture to the slow cooker, cover and
    cook on low for 7½ hours. Meanwhile, skin the fish
    fillets, if necessary, and cut the flesh into chunks. Shell
    and devein the prawns. Cut the squid bodies into rings
    and halve the tentacles or leave them whole.

4 Add the seafood to the stew, season with salt and
    pepper, re-cover and cook on high for 30 minutes,
    or until the seafood is tender and cooked through.
    Remove and discard the bay leaf, garnish the stew
    with coriander leaves and serve.

tagliatelle with tuna

ingredients

serves 4

200 g/7 oz dried egg tagliatelle
400 g/14 oz canned tuna
    steak in oil, drained
1 bunch spring onions, sliced
175 g/6 oz frozen peas
2 tsp hot chilli sauce
600 ml/1 pint hot chicken stock
115 g/4 oz grated Cheddar cheese
salt and pepper

method

1 Preheat the slow cooker, if necessary, or according to the manufacturer's instructions.

2 Bring a large saucepan of lightly salted water to the boil. Add the pasta, return to the boil and cook for 2 minutes, until the pasta ribbons are loose. Drain.

3 Break up the tuna into bite-sized chunks and place in the slow cooker with the pasta, spring onions and peas. Season to taste with salt and pepper.

4 Add the chilli sauce to the stock and pour over the ingredients in the slow cooker. Sprinkle the grated cheese over the top. Cover and cook on low for 2 hours. Serve immediately on warmed plates.

spring vegetables

ingredients

serves 4

2 tbsp olive oil

4–8 baby onions, halved

2 celery sticks, cut into
    5-mm/¼-inch slices

225 g/8 oz young carrots,
    halved if large

300 g/10½ oz new potatoes,
    halved

850 ml–1.2 litres/1½–2 pints
    vegetable stock

225 g/8 oz dried haricot beans,
    soaked overnight in cold water
    and drained

1 bouquet garni

1½–2 tbsp light soy sauce

85 g/3 oz baby sweetcorn

115 g/4 oz shelled broad beans,
    thawed if frozen

225 g/8 oz Savoy cabbage,
    shredded

1½ tbsp cornflour

salt and pepper

55–85 g/2–3 oz freshly grated
    Parmesan cheese, to serve

method

1 Preheat the slow cooker, if necessary, or according
    to the manufacturer's instructions.

2 Heat the oil in a saucepan. Add the onions, celery,
    carrots and potatoes and cook over a low heat, stirring
    frequently, for 5–8 minutes until softened. Add the
    stock, haricot beans, bouquet garni and soy sauce,
    bring to the boil, then transfer to the slow cooker.

3 Add the corn, broad beans and cabbage, season with
    salt and pepper and stir well. Cover and cook on high
    for 3–4 hours until the vegetables are tender.

4 Remove and discard the bouquet garni. Stir the
    cornflour with 3 tablespoons water to a paste in a
    small bowl, then stir into the stew. Re-cover and cook
    on high for a further 15 minutes until thickened. Serve
    the stew with the Parmesan handed separately.

vegetable hotpot with parsley dumplings

ingredients

serves 6

½ swede, cut into chunks

2 onions, sliced

2 potatoes, cut into chunks

2 carrots, cut into chunks

2 celery sticks, sliced

2 courgettes, sliced

2 tbsp tomato purée

600 ml/1 pint hot vegetable stock

1 bay leaf

1 tsp ground coriander

½ tsp dried thyme

salt and pepper

fresh coriander sprigs, to garnish

parsley dumplings

200 g/7 oz self-raising flour

115 g/4 oz vegetable suet

2 tbsp chopped fresh parsley

125 ml/4 fl oz milk

method

1 Preheat the slow cooker, if necessary, or according to the manufacturer's instructions.

2 Put the swede, onions, potatoes, carrots, celery and courgettes into the slow cooker. Stir the tomato purée into the stock and pour it over the vegetables. Add the bay leaf, ground coriander and thyme and season with salt and pepper. Cover and cook on low for 6 hours.

3 To make the dumplings, sift the flour with a pinch of salt into a bowl and stir in the suet and parsley. Add just enough milk to make a firm but light dough. Knead lightly and shape into 12 small balls.

4 Place the dumplings on top of the stew. Cook on high for 30 minutes. Remove and discard the bay leaf and garnish with coriander sprigs. Serve immediately.

winter vegetables

ingredients

serves 4

2 tbsp sunflower oil
2 onions, chopped
3 carrots, halved lengthways
3 parsnips, halved lengthways
2 bunches celery, cut into long
    chunks
2 tbsp chopped fresh parsley
1 tbsp chopped fresh coriander
300 ml/10 fl oz vegetable stock
salt and pepper

method

1 Preheat the slow cooker, if necessary, or according to the manufacturer's instructions.

2 Heat the oil in a large, heavy-based saucepan. Add the onions and cook over a medium heat, stirring occasionally, for 5 minutes until softened. Add the carrots, parsnips and celery and cook, stirring occasionally, for a further 5 minutes. Stir in the herbs, season with salt and pepper and pour in the stock. Bring to the boil.

3 Transfer the vegetable mixture to the slow cooker, cover and cook on high for 3 hours until tender. Taste and adjust the seasoning if necessary. Using a slotted spoon, transfer the vegetables to warmed plates, then spoon over a little of the cooking liquid. Garnish with a few of the reserved celery leaves.

vegetables & lentils

ingredients

serves 4

1 onion
10 cloves
225 g/8 oz Puy or green lentils
1 bay leaf
1.5 litres/2¼ pints vegetable
    stock
2 leeks, sliced
2 potatoes, diced
2 carrots, chopped
3 courgettes, sliced
1 celery stick, sliced
1 red pepper, deseeded
    and chopped
1 tbsp lemon juice
salt and pepper

method

1 Preheat the slow cooker, if necessary, or according
   to the manufacturer's instructions.

2 Peel the onion, stud it with the cloves and place it in
   the slow cooker. Add the lentils and bay leaf, pour
   in the stock, cover and cook on high for 1½ –2 hours.

3 Remove the onion with a slotted spoon and re-cover
   the slow cooker. Remove and discard the cloves and
   slice the onion. Add the onion, leeks, potatoes, carrots,
   courgettes, celery and red pepper to the lentils. Season
   with salt and pepper, re-cover and cook on high for
   3–4 hours until all the vegetables are tender.

4 Remove and discard the bay leaf and stir in the lemon
   juice. Taste and adjust the seasoning if necessary,
   then serve.

baked aubergine with courgette & tomato

ingredients

serves 4

2 large aubergines
olive oil, for brushing
2 large courgettes, sliced
4 tomatoes, sliced
1 garlic clove, finely chopped
15 g/¹/₂ oz dry breadcrumbs
15 g/¹/₂ oz grated Parmesan cheese
salt and pepper
freshly torn basil leaves,
    to garnish

method

1 Preheat the slow cooker, if necessary, or according
   to the manufacturer's instructions.

2 Cut the aubergines into fairly thin slices and brush with
   oil. Heat a large griddle pan or heavy-based frying pan
   over a high heat, then add the aubergines and cook
   in batches for 6–8 minutes, turning once, until soft
   and brown.

3 Layer the aubergines in the slow cooker with the
   courgettes, tomatoes and garlic, seasoning with salt
   and pepper between the layers.

4 Mix the breadcrumbs with the cheese and sprinkle
   over the vegetables. Cover and cook on low for
   4 hours. Serve hot, garnished with basil.

four bean chilli

ingredients

serves 4–6

2 tbsp olive oil
1 onion, chopped
2–4 garlic cloves, chopped
2 red chillies, deseeded
    and chopped
225 g/8 oz drained canned red
    kidney beans, rinsed
225 g/8 oz drained canned
    chickpeas, rinsed
225 g/8 oz drained canned
    haricot beans, rinsed
1 tbsp tomato purée
700 ml/1¼ pints vegetable stock
1 red pepper, deseeded
    and chopped
4 tomatoes, coarsely chopped
175 g/6 oz shelled broad beans,
    thawed if frozen
1 tbsp chopped fresh coriander
soured cream, to serve
sprigs of fresh coriander and pinch
    of paprika, to garnish

method

1 Preheat the slow cooker, if necessary, or according
   to the manufacturer's instructions.

2 Heat the oil in a heavy-based frying pan. Add the
   onion, garlic and chillies and cook over a low heat,
   stirring occasionally, for 5 minutes until softened. Add
   the kidney beans, chickpeas and haricot beans. Mix
   together the tomato purée with a little of the stock in
   a jug and pour it over the beans. Add the remaining
   stock and bring to the boil.

3 Transfer the mixture to the slow cooker, cover and
   cook on low for 3 hours. Stir in the red pepper,
   tomatoes, broad beans and chopped coriander,
   re-cover and cook on high for 1–1½ hours until all
   the beans are tender.

4 Serve the stew topped with spoonfuls of soured cream
   and garnished with coriander sprigs and a sprinkling
   of paprika.

entertaining

chunky beef chilli

ingredients

serves 4

250 g/9 oz dried red kidney beans,
    soaked overnight
600 ml/1 pint cold water
2 garlic cloves, chopped
5 tbsp tomato purée
1 small green chilli, chopped
2 tsp ground cumin
2 tsp ground coriander
600 g/1 lb 5 oz chuck steak, diced
1 large onion, chopped
1 large green pepper, deseeded
    and sliced
salt and pepper
soured cream, to serve

method

1 Preheat the slow cooker, if necessary, or according
   to the manufacturer's instructions.

2 Drain the beans and place in a saucepan, cover with
   cold water and bring to the boil. Boil rapidly for
   10 minutes, then remove from the heat and drain.
   Place the beans in the slow cooker and add the cold
   water to cover.

3 Mix the garlic, tomato purée, chilli, cumin and
   coriander together in a large bowl. Add the steak,
   onion and green pepper and mix to coat evenly.

4 Place the meat and vegetables on top of the beans,
   cover and cook on low for 9 hours, until the beans and
   meat are tender.

5 Stir, season to taste with salt and pepper and serve
   with soured cream.

traditional pot roast

ingredients

serves 4–6

1 onion, finely chopped
4 carrots, sliced
4 baby turnips, sliced
4 celery sticks, sliced
2 potatoes, peeled and sliced
1 sweet potato, peeled and sliced
1.3–1.8 kg/3–4 lb topside of beef
1 bouquet garni
300 ml/10 fl oz hot beef stock
salt and pepper
sprig of fresh thyme, to garnish

method.

1 Preheat the slow cooker, if necessary, or according to the manufacturer's instructions.

2 Place the onion, carrots, turnips, celery, potatoes and sweet potato in the slow cooker and stir to mix well.

3 Rub the beef all over with salt and pepper, then place on top of the bed of vegetables. Add the bouquet garni and pour in the stock. Cover and cook on low for 9–10 hours until the beef is cooked to your liking.

4 Remove the beef, carve into slices and arrange on serving plates. Remove and discard the bouquet garni. Spoon some of the vegetables and cooking juices onto the plates and serve.

duckling with apples

ingredients

serves 6

1.8–2 kg/4–4 lb 8 oz duckling,
    cut into 8 pieces
2 tbsp olive oil
1 onion, finely chopped
1 carrot, finely chopped
300 ml/10 fl oz chicken stock
300 ml/10 fl oz dry white wine
bouquet garni
4 eating apples
55 g/2 oz unsalted butter
salt and pepper

method

1 Preheat the slow cooker, if necessary, or according
   to the manufacturer's instructions.

2 Season the duckling pieces with salt and pepper. Heat
   the oil in a large, heavy-based frying pan. Add all the
   duckling pieces, placing the breast portions skin side
   down. Cook over a medium–high heat for a few
   minutes until golden brown, then transfer the breast
   portions to a plate. Turn the other pieces and continue
   to cook until browned all over. Transfer to the plate.

3 Add the onion and carrot to the frying pan and cook
   over a low heat, stirring occasionally, for 5 minutes until
   the onion is softened. Add the stock and wine and
   bring to the boil.

4 Transfer the vegetable mixture to the slow cooker. Add
   the duckling pieces and the bouquet garni. Cover and
   cook on low for 8 hours, occasionally skimming off the
   fat from the slow cooker and replacing the lid each
   time. Shortly before you are ready to serve, peel, core
   and slice the apples. Melt the butter in a large frying
   pan. Add the apple slices and cook over a medium
   heat, turning occasionally, for 5 minutes until golden.

5 Spoon the cooked apples onto warmed plates and
   divide the duckling among them. Strain the sauce
   into a jug, then pour it over the duckling and serve.

lamb tagine

ingredients

serves 6

3 tbsp olive oil
2 red onions, chopped
2 garlic cloves, finely chopped
2.5-cm/1-inch piece fresh
    ginger, finely chopped
1 yellow pepper, deseeded
    and chopped
1 kg/2 lb 4 oz boneless shoulder
    of lamb, trimmed and cut
    into 2.5-cm/1-inch cubes
850 ml/1½ pints lamb or
    chicken stock
225 g/8 oz ready-to-eat
    dried apricots, halved
1 tbsp clear honey
4 tbsp lemon juice
pinch of saffron threads
5-cm/2-inch cinnamon stick
salt and pepper
55 g/2 oz flaked almonds, toasted
sprigs of fresh coriander, to garnish

method

1 Preheat the slow cooker, if necessary, or according
   to the manufacturer's instructions.

2 Heat the oil in a large, heavy-based saucepan. Add the
   onions, garlic, ginger and yellow pepper and cook over
   a low heat, stirring occasionally, for 5 minutes until the
   onion has softened. Add the lamb and stir well to mix,
   then pour in the stock. Add the apricots, honey, lemon
   juice, saffron and cinnamon stick and season with the
   salt and pepper. Bring to the boil.

3 Transfer the mixture to the slow cooker. Cover and
   cook on low for 8½ hours until the meat is tender.

4 Remove and discard the cinnamon stick. Transfer to
   warmed serving bowls, sprinkle with the almonds,
   garnish with fresh coriander and serve.

springtime lamb with asparagus

ingredients

serves 6

2 tbsp sunflower oil
1 onion, thinly sliced
2 garlic cloves, very finely chopped
1 kg/2 lb 4 oz boneless
    shoulder of lamb, cut into
    2.5-cm/1-in cubes
225 g/8 oz asparagus spears,
    thawed if frozen
300 ml/10 fl oz chicken stock
4 tbsp lemon juice
150 ml/5 fl oz double cream
salt and pepper

method

1 Preheat the slow cooker, if necessary, or according to the manufacturer's instructions.

2 Heat the oil in a large, heavy-based frying pan. Add the onion and cook over a medium heat, stirring occasionally, for 5 minutes until softened. Add the garlic and lamb and cook, stirring occasionally, for a further 5 minutes until the lamb is lightly browned all over.

3 Meanwhile, trim off and reserve the tips of the asparagus spears. Cut the stalks into 2–3 pieces. Add the stock and lemon juice to the frying pan, season with salt and pepper and bring to the boil. Lower the heat, add the asparagus stalks and simmer for 2 minutes.

4 Transfer the mixture to the slow cooker. Cover and cook on low for 7 hours until the lamb is tender.

5 About 20 minutes before you intend to serve, cook the reserved asparagus tips in a saucepan of lightly salted boiling water for 5 minutes. Drain well, then mix with the cream. Spoon the cream mixture on top of the lamb mixture but do not stir it in. Re-cover and cook on high for 15–20 minutes to heat through before serving.

lamb shanks with olives

ingredients

serves 4

1½ tbsp plain flour
4 lamb shanks
2 tbsp olive oil
1 onion, sliced
2 garlic cloves, finely chopped
2 tsp sweet paprika
400 g/14 oz canned
    chopped tomatoes
2 tbsp tomato purée
2 carrots, sliced
2 tsp sugar
225 ml/8 fl oz red wine
5-cm/2-inch cinnamon stick
2 fresh rosemary sprigs
115 g/4 oz stoned black olives
2 tbsp lemon juice
2 tbsp chopped fresh mint
salt and pepper
fresh mint leaves, to garnish

method

1 Preheat the slow cooker, if necessary, or according to the manufacturer's instructions.

2 Spread out the flour on a plate and season with salt and pepper. Toss the lamb in the seasoned flour and shake off any excess. Heat the oil in a large, heavy-based saucepan. Add the lamb shanks and cook over a medium heat, turning frequently, for 6–8 minutes until browned all over. Transfer to a plate and set aside.

3 Add the onion and garlic to the saucepan and cook, stirring frequently, for 5 minutes until softened. Stir in the paprika and cook for 1 minute. Add the tomatoes, tomato purée, carrots, sugar, wine, cinnamon stick and rosemary and bring to the boil.

4 Transfer the vegetable mixture to the slow cooker and add the lamb shanks. Cover and cook on low for 8 hours until the lamb is very tender.

5 Add the olives, lemon juice and mint to the slow cooker. Re-cover and cook on high for 30 minutes. Remove and discard the rosemary and cinnamon and serve, garnished with mint leaves.

cinnamon lamb

ingredients

serves 6

2 tbsp plain flour
1 kg/2 lb 4 oz lean boneless
    lamb, cubed
2 tbsp olive oil
2 large onions, sliced
1 garlic clove, finely chopped
300 ml/10 fl oz red wine
2 tbsp red wine vinegar
400 g/14 oz canned
    chopped tomatoes
55 g/2 oz raisins
1 tbsp ground cinnamon
pinch of sugar
1 bay leaf
150 ml/5 fl oz Greek-style yogurt
2 garlic cloves, crushed
salt and pepper
paprika, for sprinkling

method

1 Preheat the slow cooker, if necessary, or according
   to the manufacturer's instructions.

2 Spread out the flour in a shallow dish and season with
   pepper. Add the lamb cubes and toss until well coated,
   shaking off any excess.

3 Heat the oil in a heavy-based frying pan. Add the
   onions and garlic and cook over a low heat, stirring
   occasionally, for 5 minutes until softened. Increase
   the heat to high, add the lamb and cook, stirring
   frequently, for 5 minutes until evenly browned.

4 Stir in the wine, vinegar and tomatoes with their can
   juices and bring to the boil, scraping up any sediment
   from the base of the pan. Transfer to the slow cooker,
   stir in the raisins, cinnamon, sugar and bay leaf and
   season with salt and pepper. Cover and cook on low
   for 8–8½ hours until the lamb is tender.

5 Meanwhile, prepare the topping. Mix together the
   yogurt and garlic in a small bowl and season to taste
   with salt and pepper. Cover and chill in the refrigerator
   until ready to serve.

6 Remove and discard the bay leaf. Serve each portion
   topped with a spoonful of the garlic-flavoured yogurt
   sprinkled with a little paprika.

pork with almonds

ingredients

serves 6

2 tbsp sunflower oil
2 onions, chopped
2 garlic cloves, finely chopped
5-cm/2-inch cinnamon stick
3 cloves
115 g/4 oz ground almonds
750 g/1 lb 10 oz boneless pork,
    cut into 2.5-cm/1-inch cubes
4 tomatoes, peeled and chopped
2 tbsp capers
115 g/4 oz green olives, stoned
3 pickled jalapeño chillies, drained,
    deseeded and cut into rings
350 ml/12 fl oz chicken stock
salt and pepper

method

1 Preheat the slow cooker, if necessary, or according to the manufacturer's instructions.

2 Heat half the oil in a large, heavy-based frying pan. Add the onions and cook over a low heat, stirring occasionally, for 5 minutes until softened. Add the garlic, cinnamon, cloves and almonds and cook, stirring frequently, for 8–10 minutes. Be careful not to burn the almonds.

3 Remove and discard the spices and transfer the almond mixture to a food processor. Process the mixture to a smooth purée.

4 Rinse out the pan and return to the heat. Heat the remaining oil, then add the pork, in batches if necessary. Cook over a medium heat, stirring frequently, for 5–10 minutes until browned all over. Return all the pork to the pan and add the almond purée, tomatoes, capers, olives, chillies and chicken stock. Bring to the boil, then transfer to the slow cooker.

5 Season with salt and pepper and mix well. Cover and cook on low for 5 hours. To serve, transfer to warmed plates and serve immediately.

pork & vegetable ragout

ingredients

serves 4

450 g/1 lb lean, boneless pork
1½ tbsp plain flour
1 tsp ground coriander
1 tsp ground cumin
1½ tsp ground cinnamon
1 tbsp olive oil
1 onion, chopped
400 g/14 oz canned
    chopped tomatoes
2 tbsp tomato purée
300 ml/10 fl oz chicken stock
225 g/8 oz carrots, chopped
350 g/12 oz squash, such as
    kabocha, peeled, deseeded
    and chopped
225 g/8 oz leeks, sliced, blanched
    and drained
115 g/4 oz okra, trimmed
    and sliced
salt and pepper
sprigs of fresh parsley, to garnish
couscous, to serve

method

1 Preheat the slow cooker, if necessary, or according
   to the manufacturer's instructions.

2 Trim off any visible fat from the pork and cut the meat
   into thin strips about 5 cm/2 inches long. Mix together
   the flour, coriander, cumin and cinnamon in a shallow
   dish, add the pork strips and toss well to coat. Shake
   off the excess and reserve the remaining spiced flour.

3 Heat the oil in a heavy-based frying pan. Add the
   onion and cook over a low heat, stirring occasionally,
   for 5 minutes until softened. Add the pork strips,
   increase the heat to high and cook, stirring frequently,
   for 5 minutes until browned all over. Sprinkle in the
   reserved spiced flour and cook, stirring constantly,
   for 2 minutes, then remove the pan from the heat.

4 Gradually stir in the tomatoes with their can juices.
   Combine the tomato purée with the stock in a jug,
   then gradually stir the mixture into the frying pan.
   Add the carrots, return the pan to the heat and bring
   to the boil, stirring constantly.

5 Transfer to the slow cooker, stir in the squash, leeks
   and okra, and season with salt and pepper. Cover
   and cook on low for 5–6 hours until the meat and
   vegetables are tender. Garnish with parsley sprigs and
   serve with couscous.

spicy pulled pork

ingredients

serves 4

2 onions, sliced
1.5 kg/3 lb 5 oz boned
    and rolled pork shoulder
2 tbsp demerara sugar
2 tbsp Worcestershire sauce
1 tbsp American mustard
2 tbsp tomato ketchup
1 tbsp cider vinegar
salt and pepper
hamburger buns or ciabatta
    rolls, to serve

method

1 Preheat the slow cooker, if necessary, or according
to the manufacturer's instructions.

2 Put the onions in the slow cooker and place the pork
on top. Mix the sugar, Worcestershire sauce, mustard,
ketchup and vinegar together and spread all over the
surface of the pork. Season to taste with salt and
pepper. Cover and cook on low for 8 hours.

3 Remove the pork from the slow cooker and use 2 forks
to pull it apart into shreds.

4 Skim any excess fat from the juices and stir a little
juice into the pork. Serve in hamburger buns, with
the remaining juices for spooning over the pork.

maple-glazed pork ribs

ingredients

serves 4

1 onion, finely chopped
2 plum tomatoes, diced
3 tbsp maple syrup
2 tbsp soy sauce
2 tsp hot chilli sauce
1.5 kg/3 lb 5 oz meaty pork ribs,
    cut into single ribs
salt and pepper

method

1 Preheat the slow cooker, if necessary, or according to the manufacturer's instructions.

2 Combine the onion, tomatoes, maple syrup, soy sauce, chilli sauce, and salt and pepper to taste in a large bowl. Add the pork ribs and turn to coat evenly.

3 Arrange the ribs in the slow cooker, cover and cook on high for 4 hours. If possible, turn the ribs halfway through the cooking time.

4 Lift out the ribs and place on a warmed platter. Skim the excess fat from the juices and spoon the juices over the ribs to serve.

slow roast chicken

ingredients

serves 4–6

1.5 kg/3 lb 5 oz
    oven-ready chicken
½ lemon
1 tbsp olive oil
½ tsp dried thyme
½ tsp paprika
salt and pepper

method

1 Preheat the slow cooker, if necessary, or according to the manufacturer's instructions.

2 Wipe the chicken with absorbent kitchen paper and tuck the ½ lemon inside the body cavity. Brush the oil over the chicken skin and sprinkle with thyme, paprika and salt and pepper, rubbing in with your fingers to cover all the skin.

3 Place the chicken in the slow cooker, cover and cook on high for 3 hours. Reduce the heat to low and cook for a further 4 hours, until the chicken is tender and the juices run clear when a skewer is inserted into the thickest part of the meat.

4 Carefully remove the chicken and place on a warmed platter, then skim any fat from the juices. Adjust the seasoning to taste and serve.

nutty chicken

ingredients

serves 4

3 tbsp sunflower oil
4 skinless chicken portions
2 shallots, chopped
1 tsp ground ginger
1 tbsp plain flour
425 ml/15 fl oz beef stock
55 g/2 oz walnut pieces
grated rind of 1 lemon
2 tbsp lemon juice
1 tbsp black treacle
salt and pepper
sprigs of fresh watercress,
    to garnish

method

1 Preheat the slow cooker, if necessary, or according
to the manufacturer's instructions.

2 Heat the oil in a large, heavy-based frying pan. Season
the chicken portions with salt and pepper and add to
the pan. Cook the chicken over a medium heat, turning
occasionally, for 5–8 minutes until lightly golden all
over. Transfer to the slow cooker.

3 Add the shallots to the pan and cook, stirring
occasionally, for 3–4 minutes until softened. Sprinkle in
the ginger and flour and cook, stirring constantly, for
1 minute. Gradually stir in the stock and bring to the
boil, stirring constantly. Lower the heat and simmer
for 1 minute, then stir in the nuts, lemon rind and juice
and treacle.

4 Pour the sauce over the chicken. Cover and cook on
low for 6 hours until the chicken is cooked through
and tender. Taste and adjust the seasoning if necessary.
Transfer the chicken to warmed bowls, spoon some of
the sauce over each portion, garnish with watercress
sprigs and serve immediately.

chicken cacciatore

ingredients

serves 4

3 tbsp olive oil
4 skinless chicken portions
2 onions, sliced
2 garlic cloves, finely chopped
400 g/14 oz canned
    chopped tomatoes
1 tbsp tomato purée
2 tbsp chopped fresh parsley
2 tsp fresh thyme leaves
150 ml/5 fl oz red wine
salt and pepper
sprigs of fresh thyme, to garnish

method

1 Preheat the slow cooker, if necessary, or according to the manufacturer's instructions.

2 Heat the oil in a heavy-based frying pan. Add the chicken portions and cook over a medium heat, turning occasionally, for 10 minutes until golden all over. Using a slotted spoon, transfer the chicken to the slow cooker.

3 Add the onions to the pan and cook, stirring occasionally, for 5 minutes until softened and just turning golden. Add the garlic, tomatoes and their can juices, tomato purée, parsley, thyme and wine. Season with salt and pepper and bring to the boil.

4 Pour the tomato mixture over the chicken pieces. Cover and cook on low for 5 hours until the chicken is tender and cooked through. Taste and adjust the seasoning if necessary and serve, garnished with sprigs of thyme.

chicken in riesling

ingredients

serves 4-6

2 tbsp plain flour
1 chicken, about 1.6 kg/3 lb 8 oz,
    cut into 8 pieces
55 g/2 oz unsalted butter
1 tbsp sunflower oil
4 shallots, finely chopped
12 button mushrooms, sliced
2 tbsp brandy
500 ml/18 fl oz Riesling wine
250 ml/9 fl oz double cream
salt and pepper
chopped fresh flat-leaf parsley,
    to garnish

method

1 Preheat the slow cooker, if necessary, or according to the manufacturer's instructions.

2 Put the flour in a shallow dish and season with salt and pepper. Toss the chicken pieces in the flour until well coated. Heat half the butter with the oil in a heavy-based frying pan. Add the chicken pieces and cook over a medium–high heat, turning frequently, for 10 minutes until golden all over. Transfer them to a plate.

3 Melt the remaining butter in the frying pan. Add the shallots and mushrooms and cook over a medium–high heat, stirring constantly, for 3 minutes until lightly browned. Return the chicken to the frying pan and remove it from the heat. Warm the brandy in a small ladle, ignite and pour it over the chicken, shaking the pan gently until the flames have died down.

4 Return the pan to the heat and pour in the wine. Bring to the boil over a low heat. Transfer to the slow cooker, cover and cook on low for 5–6 hours until the chicken is tender. Transfer the chicken to a serving dish and keep warm. Skim off any fat and pour the liquid into a saucepan. Stir in the cream and bring just to the boil over a low heat. Season to taste with salt and pepper and pour the sauce over the chicken. Sprinkle with chopped parsley and serve immediately.

barbecue chicken

ingredients

serves 4

8 skinless chicken drumsticks
    or thighs
3 tbsp tomato purée
2 tbsp clear honey
1 tbsp Worcestershire sauce
juice of ½ lemon
½ tsp crushed dried chillies
1 garlic clove, crushed
salt and pepper

method

1 Preheat the slow cooker, if necessary, or according to the manufacturer's instructions.

2 Using a sharp knife, cut slashes into the thickest parts of the chicken flesh.

3 Mix the tomato purée, honey, Worcestershire sauce, lemon juice, chillies and garlic together and season with salt and pepper. Add the chicken and toss well to coat evenly.

4 Arrange the chicken in the slow cooker, cover and cook on high for 3 hours.

5 Remove the chicken with a draining spoon. Skim any fat from the juices and spoon over the chicken to serve.

variation

Use a whole chicken if preferred. Clean the chicken inside and out with kitchen paper. Fry the chicken in butter in a large saucepan until brown all over. Brush the sauce over the chicken. Place in the slow cooker and cook on high for 3 hours.

seafood in saffron sauce

ingredients

serves 4

2 tbsp olive oil
1 onion, sliced
2 celery sticks, sliced
pinch of saffron threads
1 tbsp chopped fresh thyme
2 garlic cloves, finely chopped
800 g/1 lb 12 oz canned tomatoes,
    drained and chopped
175 ml/6 fl oz dry white wine
2 litres/3½ pints fish stock
225 g/8 oz live clams
225 g/8 oz live mussels
350 g/12 oz red mullet fillets
450 g/1 lb monkfish fillet
225 g/8 oz squid rings,
    thawed if frozen
2 tbsp shredded fresh basil leaves
salt and pepper

method

1 Preheat the slow cooker, if necessary, or according to the manufacturer's instructions.

2 Heat the oil in a large heavy-based saucepan. Add the onion, celery, saffron, thyme and a pinch of salt and cook over a low heat, stirring occasionally, for 5 minutes until softened. Add the garlic and cook, stirring constantly, for 2 minutes.

3 Add the tomatoes, wine and stock, season with salt and pepper and bring to the boil, stirring constantly. Transfer the mixture to the slow cooker, cover and cook on low for 5 hours.

4 Meanwhile, scrub the shellfish under cold running water and pull the 'beards' off the mussels. Discard any with broken shells or that do not shut immediately when sharply tapped. Cut the mullet and monkfish fillets into bite-sized chunks.

5 Add the pieces of fish, the shellfish and the squid rings to the slow cooker, re-cover and cook on high for 30 minutes until the clams and mussels have opened and the fish is cooked through. Discard any shellfish that remain closed. Stir in the basil and serve.

mixed mediterranean shellfish

ingredients

serves 8

1 tbsp olive oil
115 g/4 oz bacon, diced
2 tbsp butter
2 shallots, chopped
2 leeks, sliced
2 celery sticks, chopped
2 potatoes, diced
675 g/1 lb 8 oz tomatoes, peeled,
    deseeded and chopped
3 tbsp chopped fresh parsley
3 tbsp snipped fresh chives,
    plus extra to garnish
1 bay leaf
1 fresh thyme sprig
1.4 litres/2½ pints fish stock
24 live mussels
24 live clams
450 g/1 lb sea bream fillets
24 raw tiger prawns
salt and pepper

method

1 Preheat the slow cooker, if necessary, or according to the manufacturer's instructions.

2 Heat the oil in a heavy-based frying pan. Add the bacon and cook, stirring frequently, for 5–8 minutes until crisp. Using a slotted spoon, transfer to the slow cooker. Add the butter to the frying pan and when it has melted, add the shallots, leeks, celery and potatoes. Cook over a low heat, stirring occasionally, for 5 minutes until softened. Stir in the tomatoes, parsley, chives, bay leaf and thyme, pour in the stock and bring to the boil, stirring constantly. Pour the mixture into the slow cooker, cover and cook on low for 7 hours.

3 Meanwhile, scrub the mussels and clams under cold running water and pull off the 'beards' from the mussels. Discard any with broken shells or that do not shut immediately when sharply tapped. Cut the fish fillets into bite-size chunks. Peel and devein the prawns.

4 Remove and discard the bay leaf and thyme sprig from the stew. Season with salt and pepper and add all the fish and seafood. Re-cover and cook on high for 30 minutes. Discard any shellfish that remain closed. Serve garnished with extra chives.

french-style fish

ingredients

serves 4–6

1 prepared squid
900 g/2 lb mixed white fish,
    such as sea bass, monkfish,
    red mullet and grouper, filleted,
    and cut into chunks
24 large raw prawns, peeled and
    deveined, reserving heads and
    shells tied in muslin
2 tbsp olive oil
1 large onion, finely chopped
1 fennel bulb, thinly sliced,
    feathery fronds reserved
2 large garlic cloves, crushed
4 tbsp Pernod
large pinch of saffron threads,
    freshly toasted
1 litre/1¾ pints fish stock
2 large tomatoes, peeled, deseeded
    and diced, or 400 g/14 oz
    canned chopped tomatoes,
    drained
1 tbsp tomato purée
1 bay leaf
pinch of sugar
pinch of dried chilli flakes
    (optional)
salt and pepper

method

1 Preheat the slow cooker, if necessary, or according
   to the manufacturer's instructions.

2 Cut off and reserve the tentacles from the squid and
   slice the body into 5-mm/¼-inch rings. Place the
   seafood in a bowl, cover and chill in the refrigerat
   until required.

3 Heat the oil in a heavy-based frying pan. Add the
   onion and fennel and cook over a low heat, stirring
   occasionally, for 5 minutes until softened. Add the
   garlic and cook, stirring frequently, for 2 minutes.
   Remove the pan from the heat. Heat the Pernod in
   a ladle or small saucepan, ignite and pour it over the
   onion and fennel, gently shaking the frying pan until
   the flames have died down.

4 Return the frying pan to the heat, stir in the toasted
   saffron, stock, tomatoes, tomato purée, bay leaf, sugar
   and chilli flakes, if using, and season with salt and
   pepper. Bring to the boil, then transfer to the slow
   cooker, add the bag of prawn shells, cover and cook
   on low for 6 hours.

5 Remove and discard the bag of prawn shells and the
   bay leaf. Add the fish and seafood to the slow cooker,
   cover and cook on high for 30 minutes. Serve
   garnished with the reserved fennel fronds.

pollock bake

ingredients

serves 4

1 tbsp olive oil
1 red onion, sliced
1 yellow pepper, deseeded
    and sliced
4 pollock fillets, about
    140 g/5 oz each
2 tomatoes, thinly sliced
8 stoned black olives, halved
1 garlic clove, thinly sliced
2 tsp balsamic vinegar
juice of 1 orange
salt and pepper

method

1 Preheat the slow cooker, if necessary, or according to the manufacturer's instructions.

2 Heat the oil in a frying pan, add the onion and yellow pepper and fry over a high heat for 3–4 minutes, stirring, until lightly browned. Transfer to the slow cooker, cover and cook on high for 1 hour.

3 Arrange the fish fillets over the vegetables and season with salt and pepper. Arrange a layer of tomatoes and olives over the top and sprinkle with the garlic, vinegar and salt and pepper. Pour over the orange juice, cover and cook on high for a further 1 hour. Serve immediately.

poached salmon
with dill & lime

ingredients

serves 4

30 g/1 oz butter, melted
1 onion, thinly sliced
450 g/1 lb potatoes, peeled
    and thinly sliced
100 ml/3½ fl oz hot fish stock
    or water
4 pieces skinless salmon fillet,
    about 140 g/5 oz each
juice of 1 lime
2 tbsp chopped fresh dill
salt and pepper
lime wedges, to serve

method

1 Preheat the slow cooker, if necessary, or according
   to the manufacturer's instructions.

2 Brush the base of the slow cooker with 1 tablespoon
   of the butter. Layer the onion and potatoes in the slow
   cooker, sprinkling with salt and pepper between the
   layers. Add the stock and dot with 1 tablespoon of the
   butter. Cover and cook on low for 3 hours.

3 Arrange the salmon over the vegetables in a single
   layer. Drizzle the lime juice over, sprinkle with dill and
   salt and pepper and pour the remaining butter on top.
   Cover and cook on low for a further 1 hour, until the
   fish flakes easily.

4 Serve the salmon and vegetables on warmed plates
   with the juices spooned over and lime wedges on
   the side.

baked asparagus
& spinach risotto

ingredients

serves 4

2 tbsp olive oil
4 shallots, finely chopped
280 g/10 oz arborio rice
1 garlic clove, crushed
100 ml/3½ fl oz dry white wine
850 ml/1½ pints hot chicken stock
    or vegetable stock
200 g/7 oz asparagus spears
200 g/7 oz baby spinach leaves
40 g/1½ oz finely grated
    Parmesan cheese
salt and pepper

method

1 Preheat the slow cooker, if necessary, or according
    to the manufacturer's instructions.

2 Heat the oil in a frying pan, add the shallots and fry
    over a medium heat, stirring, for 2–3 minutes. Add the
    rice and garlic and cook for a further 2 minutes, stirring.
    Add the wine and allow it to boil for 30 seconds.

3 Transfer the rice mixture to the slow cooker, add the
    stock and season to taste with salt and pepper. Cover
    and cook on high for 2 hours, or until most of the liquid
    is absorbed.

4 Cut the asparagus into 4.5-cm/1¾-inch lengths.
    Stir into the rice, then spread the spinach over the
    top. Replace the lid and cook on high for a further
    30 minutes, until the asparagus is just tender and
    the spinach is wilted.

5 Stir in the spinach with the Parmesan cheese, then
    adjust the seasoning to taste and serve immediately
    in warmed bowls.

tuscan beans

ingredients

serves 4

1 large fennel bulb

2 tbsp olive oil

1 red onion, cut into small wedges

2–4 garlic cloves, sliced

1 green chilli, deseeded
and chopped

1 aubergine, about 225 g/8 oz,
cut into chunks

2 tbsp tomato purée

450 ml/16 fl oz vegetable stock

450 g/1 lb tomatoes, sliced

1 tbsp balsamic vinegar

4 fresh oregano sprigs

400 g/14 oz canned borlotti
beans, drained and rinsed

400 g/14 oz canned flageolet
beans, drained and rinsed

1 yellow pepper, deseeded and cut
into small strips

1 courgette, halved lengthways
and sliced

55 g/2 oz stoned black olives

salt and pepper

25 g/1 oz Parmesan cheese,
to garnish

method

1 Preheat the slow cooker, if necessary, or according
to the manufacturer's instructions.

2 Trim the fennel bulb, reserving the feathery fronds,
then cut the bulb into thin strips. Heat the oil in a
heavy-based frying pan. Add the fennel strips, onion,
garlic and chilli and cook over a low heat, stirring
occasionally, for 5–8 minutes until softened. Add the
aubergine and cook, stirring frequently, for 5 minutes.

3 Mix together the tomato purée and half the stock in
a jug and add to the frying pan. Pour in the remaining
stock, add the tomatoes, vinegar and oregano and
bring to the boil, stirring constantly.

4 Transfer the mixture to the slow cooker. Stir in the
beans, yellow pepper, courgette and olives and season
with salt and pepper. Cover and cook on high for
3–4 hours, until all the vegetables are tender.

5 Taste and adjust the seasoning if necessary. Thinly
shave the Parmesan over the top of the stew, garnish
with the reserved fennel fronds and serve.

mixed bean chilli

ingredients

serves 4–6

2 tbsp sunflower oil

1 onion, chopped

1 garlic clove, finely chopped

1 fresh red chilli, deseeded
    and chopped

1 yellow pepper, deseeded
    and chopped

1 tsp ground cumin

1 tbsp chilli powder

115 g/4 oz dried red kidney beans,
    soaked overnight, drained
    and rinsed

115 g/4 oz dried black beans,
    soaked overnight, drained
    and rinsed

115 g/4 oz dried pinto beans,
    soaked overnight, drained
    and rinsed

1 litre/1¾ pints vegetable stock

1 tbsp sugar

salt and pepper

chopped fresh coriander,
    to garnish

method

1 Preheat the slow cooker, if necessary, or according
to the manufacturer's instructions.

2 Heat the oil in a large, heavy-based saucepan. Add the
onion, garlic, chilli and yellow pepper and cook over a
medium heat, stirring occasionally, for 5 minutes. Stir
in the cumin and chilli powder and cook, stirring, for
1–2 minutes. Add the drained beans and stock and
bring to the boil. Boil vigorously for 15 minutes.

3 Transfer the mixture to the slow cooker, cover and
cook on low for 10 hours until the beans are tender.

4 Season the mixture with salt and pepper, then ladle
about one-third into a bowl. Mash well with a potato
masher, then return the mashed beans to the slow
cooker and stir in the sugar. Serve immediately,
sprinkled with chopped fresh coriander.

mixed vegetables

ingredients

serves 4

500 g/1 lb 2 oz potatoes,
　　peeled and cubed
2 courgettes, cubed
2 red peppers, deseeded
　　and cubed
2 red onions, sliced
2 tsp mixed dried herbs
250 ml/9 fl oz hot vegetable stock
salt and pepper

method

1 Preheat the slow cooker, if necessary, or according
　to the manufacturer's instructions.

2 Layer all the vegetables in the slow cooker, sprinkling
　with herbs and salt and pepper between the layers.

3 Pour over the stock. Cover and cook on low for 7 hours.
　Serve in warmed bowls.

around
the world

brunswick chicken

ingredients

serves 6

1.8 kg/4 lb chicken portions
2 tbsp paprika
2 tbsp olive oil
2 tbsp butter
450 g/1 lb onions, chopped
2 yellow peppers, deseeded
    and chopped
400 g/14 oz canned chopped
    tomatoes
225 ml/8 fl oz dry white wine
450 ml/16 fl oz chicken stock
1 tbsp Worcestershire sauce
½ tsp Tabasco sauce
1 tbsp finely chopped fresh parsley
2 tbsp plain flour
325 g/11½ oz canned sweetcorn
    kernels, drained
425 g/15 oz canned butter beans,
    drained and rinsed
salt
sprigs of fresh parsley, to garnish

method

1 Preheat the slow cooker, if necessary, or according
   to the manufacturer's instructions.

2 Season the chicken portions with salt and dust with
   the paprika. Heat the oil and butter in a heavy-based
   frying pan. Add the chicken portions and cook over a
   medium–high heat, turning frequently, for 10 minutes
   until golden brown all over. Using a slotted spoon,
   transfer the chicken to the slow cooker.

3 Add the onions and peppers to the frying pan, lower
   the heat and cook, stirring occasionally, for 5 minutes
   until softened. Add the tomatoes with their can juices,
   wine, stock, Worcestershire sauce, Tabasco sauce and
   chopped parsley and bring to the boil, stirring
   constantly. Pour the mixture over the chicken, cover
   and cook on low for 5 hours.

4 Mix the flour with 4 tablespoons of water to a paste in
   a small, heatproof bowl. Add a ladleful of the cooking
   liquid and mix well, then stir the mixture into the stew.
   Add the sweetcorn and butter beans, re-cover and
   cook on high for 30 minutes until the chicken is
   tender and cooked through. Serve garnished with
   parsley sprigs.

chipotle chicken

ingredients

serves 4

4–6 dried chipotle chillies
4 garlic cloves, unpeeled
1 small onion, chopped
400 g/14 oz canned
    chopped tomatoes
300 ml/10 fl oz hot chicken
    or vegetable stock
4 skinless chicken breasts
salt and pepper
chopped fresh flat-leaf parsley,
    to garnish

method.

1 Preheat the oven to 200°C/400°F/Gas Mark 6. Place the chillies in a bowl and pour in just enough hot water to cover. Set aside to soak for 30 minutes. Meanwhile, place the unpeeled garlic cloves on a baking sheet and roast in the oven for about 10 minutes until soft. Remove from the oven and set aside to cool.

2 Drain the chillies, reserving 125 ml/4 fl oz of the soaking water. Deseed the chillies, if you like, and chop coarsely. Place the chillies and reserved soaking water in a blender or food processor and process to a purée. Peel and mash the garlic in a bowl.

3 Preheat the slow cooker, if necessary, or according to the manufacturer's instructions.

4 Place the chilli purée, garlic, onion and tomatoes in the slow cooker and stir in the stock. Season the chicken portions with salt and pepper and place them in the slow cooker. Cover and cook on low for about 5 hours until the chicken is tender and cooked through.

5 Lift the chicken out of the slow cooker with a slotted spoon, cover and keep warm. Pour the cooking liquid into a saucepan and bring to the boil on the hob. Boil for 5–10 minutes until reduced. Place the chicken on warmed plates, spoon the sauce over it, garnish with the chopped parsley and serve.

florida chicken

ingredients

serves 4

1½ tbsp plain flour
450 g/1 lb skinless, boneless
    chicken, cut into bite-sized
    pieces
1 tbsp olive oil
1 onion, cut into wedges
2 celery sticks, sliced
150 ml/5 fl oz orange juice
300 ml/10 fl oz chicken stock
1 tbsp light soy sauce
1–2 tsp clear honey
1 tbsp grated orange rind
1 orange pepper, deseeded
    and chopped
225 g/8 oz courgettes, halved
    lengthways and sliced
2 corn on the cobs, cut into chunks
1 orange, peeled and segmented
salt and pepper
1 tbsp chopped fresh parsley,
    to garnish

method

1 Preheat the slow cooker, if necessary, or according
   to the manufacturer's instructions.

2 Spread out the flour in a shallow dish and season with
   salt and pepper. Add the chicken and toss well to coat,
   shaking off any excess. Reserve the remaining
   seasoned flour.

3 Heat the oil in a heavy-based frying pan. Add the
   chicken and cook over a high heat, stirring frequently,
   for 5 minutes until golden brown all over. Using a
   slotted spoon, transfer the chicken to the slow cooker.

4 Add the onion and celery to the frying pan, lower the
   heat and cook, stirring occasionally, for 5 minutes until
   softened. Sprinkle in the reserved seasoned flour and
   cook, stirring constantly, for 2 minutes. Remove the
   pan from the heat. Gradually stir in the orange juice,
   stock, soy sauce and honey, then add the orange rind.
   Return the pan to the heat and bring to the boil,
   stirring constantly.

5 Pour the mixture over the chicken and add the orange
   pepper, courgettes and corn on the cobs. Cover and
   cook on low for 5 hours until the chicken is tender and
   cooked through. Stir in the orange segments, re-cover
   and cook on high for 15 minutes. Serve garnished with
   the parsley.

chicken italian-style

ingredients

serves 4

1 tbsp plain flour
4 chicken portions, about
    175 g/6 oz each
2½ tbsp olive oil
8–12 shallots, halved if large
2–4 garlic cloves, sliced
400 ml/14 fl oz chicken stock
50 ml/2 fl oz dry sherry
4 fresh thyme sprigs
115 g/4 oz cherry tomatoes
115 g/4 oz baby sweetcorn,
    halved lengthways
2 slices white or wholemeal bread,
    crusts removed, cubed
salt and pepper
1 tbsp chopped fresh thyme,
    to garnish

method

1 Preheat the slow cooker, if necessary, or according
   to the manufacturer's instructions.

2 Spread out the flour in a shallow dish and season with
   salt and pepper. Add the chicken portions and toss well
   to coat, shaking off any excess. Reserve the remaining
   seasoned flour. Heat 1 tablespoon of the oil in a
   heavy-based frying pan. Add the chicken portions and
   cook over a medium–high heat, turning frequently, for
   10 minutes until golden brown all over. Using a slotted
   spoon, transfer the chicken to the slow cooker.

3 Add the shallots and garlic to the frying pan, lower the
   heat and cook, stirring occasionally, for 5 minutes until
   softened. Sprinkle in the reserved seasoned flour and
   cook, stirring constantly, for 2 minutes. Remove from
   the heat and gradually stir in the stock and sherry, then
   bring to the boil, stirring constantly. Pour the mixture
   over the chicken and add the thyme sprigs, tomatoes
   and baby sweetcorn. Cover and cook on low for 5–6
   hours until the chicken is tender and cooked through.

4 Meanwhile, heat the remaining oil in a frying pan,
   add the bread cubes and cook, stirring frequently, for
   4–5 minutes until golden all over. Remove and discard
   the thyme sprigs from the stew, then serve, garnished
   with the croûtons and chopped thyme.

bulgarian chicken

ingredients

serves 6

4 tbsp sunflower oil
6 chicken portions
2 onions, chopped
2 garlic cloves, finely chopped
1 fresh red chilli, deseeded and
    finely chopped
6 tomatoes, peeled and chopped
2 tsp sweet paprika
1 bay leaf
225 ml/8 fl oz hot chicken stock
salt and pepper

method

1 Preheat the slow cooker, if necessary, or according to the manufacturer's instructions.

2 Heat the oil in a large, heavy-based frying pan. Add the chicken portions and cook over a medium heat, turning occasionally, for about 10 minutes, until golden all over.

3 Transfer the contents of the pan to the slow cooker and add the onions, garlic, chilli and tomatoes. Sprinkle in the paprika, add the bay leaf and pour in the stock. Season with salt and pepper. Stir well, cover and cook on low for 6 hours until the chicken is cooked through and tender. Remove and discard the bay leaf, then serve immediately.

easy chinese chicken

ingredients

serves 4

2 tsp grated fresh ginger
4 garlic cloves, finely chopped
2 star anise
150 ml/5 fl oz Chinese rice wine
    or medium dry sherry
2 tbsp dark soy sauce
1 tsp sesame oil
4 skinless chicken thighs or
    drumsticks
shredded spring onions, to garnish
boiled rice, to serve

method

1 Preheat the slow cooker, if necessary, or according to the manufacturer's instructions.

2 Mix together the ginger, garlic, star anise, rice wine, soy sauce and sesame oil in a bowl and stir in 5 tablespoons of water. Place the chicken in a saucepan, add the spice mixture and bring to the boil.

3 Transfer the mixture to the slow cooker, cover and cook on low for 4 hours or until the chicken is tender and cooked through.

4 Remove and discard the star anise. Transfer the chicken to warmed plates and serve garnished with shredded spring onions with boiled rice.

jambalaya-style duckling

ingredients

serves 4

4 duckling breasts, about
     175 g/6 oz each
2 tbsp olive oil
225 g/8 oz gammon,
     cut into small chunks
225 g/8 oz chorizo or other spicy
     sausages, skinned and sliced
1 onion, chopped
3 garlic cloves, chopped
3 celery sticks, chopped
1–2 red chillies, deseeded
     and chopped
1 green pepper, deseeded
     and chopped
600 ml/1 pint chicken stock
1 tbsp chopped fresh oregano
400 g/14 oz canned chopped
     tomatoes
1–2 tsp hot pepper sauce
fresh parsley sprigs, to garnish
green salad and boiled rice,
     to serve

method

1 Preheat the slow cooker, if necessary, or according
   to the manufacturer's instructions.

2 Remove and discard the skin and any visible fat from
   the duckling breasts and cut the flesh into bite-sized
   pieces. Heat half the oil in a heavy-based frying pan,
   add the duckling, gammon and chorizo and cook over
   a high heat, stirring frequently, for 5 minutes until
   browned all over. Using a slotted spoon, transfer the
   meat to the slow cooker.

3 Add the onion, garlic, celery and chilli to the frying
   pan, lower the heat and cook, stirring occasionally, for
   5 minutes until softened. Add the green pepper and
   stir in the stock, oregano, tomatoes with the can juices
   and hot pepper sauce. Bring to the boil, then pour the
   mixture over the meat.

4 Cover the slow cooker and cook the jambalaya on low
   for 6 hours, until the meat is tender. Serve garnished
   with parsley sprigs and accompanied by a green salad
   and boiled rice.

mexican pork chops

ingredients

serves 4

4 pork chops, trimmed of excess fat
2 tbsp sunflower oil
450 g/1 lb canned pineapple
    cubes in fruit juice
1 red pepper, deseeded
    and finely chopped
2 fresh jalapeño chillies,
    deseeded and finely chopped
1 onion, finely chopped
1 tbsp chopped fresh coriander
125 ml/4 fl oz hot chicken stock
salt and pepper
sprigs of fresh coriander,
    to garnish
tortillas, to serve

method

1 Preheat the slow cooker, if necessary, or according
to the manufacturer's instructions.

2 Season the chops with salt and pepper. Heat the oil in a
large, heavy-based frying pan. Add the chops and cook
over a medium heat for 2–3 minutes each side until
lightly browned. Transfer them to the slow cooker.
Drain the pineapple, reserving the juice, and set aside.

3 Add the red pepper, chillies and onion to the frying
pan and cook, stirring occasionally, for 5 minutes until
the onion is softened. Transfer the mixture to the slow
cooker and add the coriander and stock, together with
125 ml/4 fl oz of the reserved pineapple juice. Cover
and cook on low for 6 hours until the chops are tender.

4 Add the reserved pineapple to the slow cooker,
re-cover and cook on high for 15 minutes. Garnish
with fresh coriander sprigs and serve immediately,
with tortillas.

poor man's cassoulet

ingredients

serves 4

2 tbsp sunflower oil
2 onions, chopped
2 garlic cloves, finely chopped
115 g/4 oz streaky bacon,
    derinded and chopped
500 g/1 lb 2 oz pork sausages
400 g/14 oz canned haricot,
    red kidney or black-eyed
    beans, drained and rinsed
2 tbsp chopped fresh parsley
150 ml/5 fl oz hot beef stock
4 slices French bread and
    55 g/2 oz grated Gruyère
    cheese, to serve

method

1 Preheat the slow cooker, if necessary, or according
to the manufacturer's instructions.

2 Heat the oil in a heavy-based frying pan. Add the
onions and cook over a low heat, stirring occasionally,
for 5 minutes until softened. Add the garlic, bacon and
sausages and cook, stirring and turning the sausages
occasionally, for a further 5 minutes.

3 Using a slotted spoon, transfer the mixture from the
frying pan to the slow cooker. Add the beans, parsley
and beef stock, then cover and cook on low for
6 hours.

4 Preheat the grill to high. Just before serving, lightly
toast the bread under the grill. Divide the grated
cheese between the toast slices and place under the
grill until just melted.

5 Ladle the stew onto warmed plates, top each portion
with the cheese-toast and serve.

jambalaya

ingredients

serves 6

½ tsp cayenne pepper

½ tsp freshly ground
black pepper

1 tsp salt

2 tsp chopped fresh thyme

350 g/12 oz skinless, boneless
chicken breasts, diced

2 tbsp sunflower oil

2 onions, chopped

2 garlic cloves, finely chopped

2 green peppers, deseeded
and chopped

2 celery sticks, chopped

115 g/4 oz smoked ham, chopped

175 g/6 oz chorizo sausage,
skinned and sliced

400 g/14 oz canned
chopped tomatoes

2 tbsp tomato purée

225 ml/8 fl oz chicken stock

450 g/1 lb peeled raw prawns

450 g/1 lb cooked rice

snipped fresh chives, to garnish

method

1 Preheat the slow cooker, if necessary, or according to the manufacturer's instructions.

2 Mix together the cayenne, black pepper, salt and thyme in a bowl. Add the chicken and toss to coat. Heat the oil in a large, heavy-based saucepan. Add the onions, garlic, green peppers and celery and cook over a low heat, stirring occasionally, for 5 minutes. Add the chicken and cook over a medium heat, stirring frequently, for a further 5 minutes until golden all over. Stir in the ham, chorizo, tomatoes, tomato purée and stock and bring to the boil.

3 Transfer the mixture to the slow cooker. Cover and cook on low for 6 hours. Add the prawns and rice, re-cover and cook on high for 30 minutes.

4 Taste and adjust the seasoning, if necessary. Transfer to warm plates, garnish with chives and serve the jambalaya immediately.

oriental pork

ingredients

serves 4

450 g/1 lb lean boneless pork
1½ tbsp plain flour
1–2 tbsp groundnut oil
1 onion, cut into small wedges
2–3 garlic cloves, chopped
2.5-cm/1-inch piece fresh ginger,
    grated
1 red pepper, deseeded and sliced
1 green pepper, deseeded
    and sliced
1 tbsp tomato purée
300 ml/10 fl oz chicken stock
225 g/8 oz canned pineapple
    chunks in natural juice
1–1½ tbsp dark soy sauce
1½ tbsp rice vinegar
4 spring onions, diagonally sliced,
    to garnish
rice, to serve

method

1 Preheat the slow cooker, if necessary, or according
   to the manufacturer's instructions.

2 Trim off all visible fat from the pork and cut the meat
   into 2.5-cm/1-inch chunks. Spread out the flour in
   a shallow dish, add the pork and toss well to coat,
   shaking off any excess. Reserve the remaining flour.

3 Heat the oil in a heavy-based frying pan. Add the
   onion, garlic, ginger and peppers and cook over a low
   heat, stirring occasionally, for 5 minutes until softened.
   Add the pork, increase the heat and cook, stirring
   frequently, for 5 minutes until browned all over.
   Sprinkle in the reserved flour and cook, stirring
   constantly, for 2 minutes, then remove the pan from
   the heat.

4 Mix the tomato purée and stock in a jug, then gradually
   stir into the frying pan. Drain the pineapple, reserving
   the juice. Stir the juice and soy sauce into the pan.
   Return the pan to the heat and bring to the boil,
   stirring constantly. Transfer to the slow cooker, cover
   and cook on low for 5–6 hours.

5 Stir in the pineapple and vinegar, re-cover and cook
   on high for 30 minutes. Garnish with the sliced spring
   onions and serve with rice.

neapolitan beef

ingredients

serves 6

300 ml/10 fl oz red wine
4 tbsp olive oil
1 celery stick, chopped
2 shallots, sliced
4 garlic cloves, finely chopped
1 bay leaf
10 fresh basil leaves, plus extra
    to garnish
3 fresh parsley sprigs
pinch of grated nutmeg
pinch of ground cinnamon
2 cloves
1.5 kg/3 lb 5 oz beef silverside
1–2 garlic cloves, thinly sliced
55 g/2 oz streaky bacon or
    pancetta, derinded and
    chopped
400g/14 oz canned chopped
    tomatoes
2 tbsp tomato purée

method

1 Preheat the slow cooker, if necessary, or according to the manufacturer's instructions.

2 Combine the wine, 2 tablespoons of the olive oil, the celery, shallots, garlic, herbs and spices in a large, non-metallic bowl. Add the beef, cover and marinate, turning occasionally, for 12 hours.

3 Drain the beef, reserving the marinade, and pat dry with kitchen paper. Make small incisions all over the beef using a sharp knife. Insert a slice of garlic and a piece of bacon in each 'pocket'. Heat the remaining oil in a large frying pan. Add the meat and cook over a medium heat, turning frequently, until browned all over. Transfer to the slow cooker.

4 Strain the reserved marinade into the frying pan and bring to the boil. Stir in the tomatoes and tomato purée. Stir well, then pour the mixture over the beef. Cover and cook on low for about 9 hours until tender. If possible, turn the beef over halfway through the cooking time. To serve, remove the beef and place on a carving board. Cover with foil and leave to stand for 10–15 minutes to firm up. Cut into slices and transfer to a platter. Spoon over the sauce, garnish with basil and serve immediately.

caribbean beef

ingredients

serves 6

450 g/1 lb braising steak
450 g/1 lb diced pumpkin
  or other squash
1 onion, chopped
1 red pepper, deseeded
  and chopped
2 garlic cloves, finely chopped
2.5-cm/1-inch piece fresh ginger,
  finely chopped
1 tbsp sweet or hot paprika
225 ml/8 fl oz beef stock
400 g/14 oz canned chopped
  tomatoes
400 g/14 oz canned pigeon peas,
  drained and rinsed
400 g/14 oz canned black-eyed
  beans, drained and rinsed

method

1 Preheat the slow cooker, if necessary, or according to the manufacturer's instructions.

2 Trim off any visible fat from the steak, then dice the meat. Heat a large, heavy-based saucepan without adding any extra fat. Add the meat and cook, stirring constantly, for a few minutes until golden all over. Stir in the pumpkin, onion, red pepper, garlic and ginger and cook for 1 minute, then add the paprika, stock and tomatoes and bring to the boil.

3 Transfer the mixture to the slow cooker, cover and cook on low for 7 hours. Add the pigeon peas and black-eyed beans to the stew and season to taste with salt and pepper. Re-cover and cook on high for 30 minutes, then serve.

beef bourguinon

ingredients

serves 6

6 rashers streaky bacon,
    derinded and chopped
2 tbsp plain flour
900 g/2 lb braising steak,
    trimmed and cut into
    2.5-cm/1-inch cubes
3 tbsp olive oil
25 g/1 oz unsalted butter
12 baby onions or shallots
2 garlic cloves, finely chopped
150 ml/5 fl oz beef stock
450 ml/16 fl oz full-bodied
    red wine
1 bouquet garni
140 g/5 oz mushrooms, sliced
salt and pepper

method

1 Preheat the slow cooker, if necessary, or according
   to the manufacturer's instructions.

2 Cook the bacon in a large, heavy-based saucepan,
   stirring occasionally, until the fat runs and the pieces
   are crisp. Meanwhile, spread out the flour on a plate
   and season with salt and pepper. Toss the steak cubes
   in the flour to coat, shaking off any excess. Using a
   slotted spoon, transfer the bacon to a plate. Add the oil
   to the saucepan. When it is hot, add the steak cubes
   and cook, in batches, stirring occasionally, for 5 minutes
   until browned all over. Transfer to the plate with a
   slotted spoon.

3 Add the butter to the saucepan. When it has melted, add
   the onions and garlic and cook, stirring occasionally,
   for 5 minutes. Return the bacon and steak to the pan
   and pour in the stock and wine. Bring to the boil.

4 Transfer the mixture to the slow cooker and add the
   bouquet garni. Cover and cook on low for 7 hours until
   the meat is tender.

5 Add the mushrooms to the slow cooker and stir well.
   Re-cover and cook on high for 15 minutes. Remove
   and discard the bouquet garni. Adjust the seasoning
   if necessary, then serve immediately.

mediterranean lamb with apricots & pistachio nuts

ingredients

serves 4

1½ tbsp plain flour
1 tsp ground coriander
½ tsp ground cumin
½ tsp ground allspice
450 g/1 lb boneless lamb leg
    steaks, trimmed and cut into
    2.5-cm/1-inch chunks
1 tbsp olive oil
1 onion, chopped
2–3 garlic cloves, chopped
450 ml/16 fl oz lamb or
    chicken stock
pinch of saffron threads, infused
    in 2 tbsp water
1 cinnamon stick
85 g/3 oz dried apricots, chopped
175 g/6 oz courgettes, sliced
115 g/4 oz cherry tomatoes
1 tbsp chopped fresh coriander
salt and pepper
2 tbsp coarsely chopped
    pistachio nuts, to garnish
couscous or rice, to serve

method

1 Preheat the slow cooker, if necessary, or according to the manufacturer's instructions.

2 Mix together the flour, ground coriander, cumin and allspice in a shallow dish, add the lamb and toss until well coated. Reserve the remaining spiced flour.

3 Heat the oil in a heavy-based frying pan. Add the onion and garlic and cook over a low heat, stirring occasionally, for 5 minutes until softened. Add the lamb, increase the heat to high and cook, stirring frequently, for 3 minutes until browned. Sprinkle in the reserved spiced flour and cook, stirring constantly, for 2 minutes, then remove the pan from the heat.

4 Gradually stir in the stock and the saffron with its soaking liquid. Return the pan to the heat and bring to the boil, stirring constantly. Transfer the mixture to the slow cooker and add the cinnamon stick, apricots, courgettes and tomatoes. Cover and cook on low for 8 hours until the meat is tender.

5 Remove and discard the cinnamon stick. Stir in the chopped coriander, season to taste with salt and pepper, sprinkle with the pistachio nuts and serve with couscous or rice.

bouillabaisse

ingredients

serves 6

2.25 kg/5 lb mixed white fish,
    such as red mullet, sea bream,
    sea bass, monkfish and
    whiting, filleted with bones
    and heads reserved, if possible
450 g/1 lb raw prawns, peeled
    and deveined, shells and heads
    reserved, if possible
grated rind of 1 orange
pinch of saffron threads
4 garlic cloves, finely chopped
225 ml/8 fl oz olive oil
2 onions, finely chopped
1 leek, thinly sliced
4 potatoes, thinly sliced
2 large tomatoes,
    peeled and chopped
1 bunch fresh flat-leaf
    parsley, chopped
1 fresh fennel sprig
1 fresh thyme sprig
1 bay leaf
2 cloves
6 black peppercorns
1 strip orange rind
sea salt
crusty bread or croûtes, to serve

method

1 Preheat the slow cooker, if necessary, or according
   to the manufacturer's instructions.

2 Cut the fish fillets into bite-sized pieces. Place the
   chunks of fish and the prawns in a large bowl. Sprinkle
   with the grated orange rind, saffron, half the garlic
   and 2 tablespoons of the oil. Cover and set aside in
   the refrigerator.

3 Put the remaining garlic, the onions, leek, potatoes,
   tomatoes, parsley, fennel, thyme, bay leaf, cloves,
   peppercorns and strip of orange rind in the slow
   cooker. Add the fish heads and bones, if using, and the
   prawn shells and heads. Pour in the remaining olive oil
   and 2.8 litres/5 pints boiling water or enough to cover
   the ingredients by 2.5 cm/1 inch. Season with sea salt.
   Cover and cook on low for 8 hours.

4 Strain the stock and return the liquid to the slow
   cooker. Discard the flavourings, fish and prawn
   trimmings but retain the vegetables and return them
   to the slow cooker if you like. Add the fish and prawn
   mixture, re-cover and cook on high for 30 minutes
   until the fish is cooked through and flakes easily.

5 Ladle into warm bowls and serve with crusty bread
   or croûtes.

moroccan sea bream

ingredients

serves 2

2 tbsp olive oil
2 onions, chopped
2 garlic cloves, finely chopped
2 carrots, finely chopped
1 fennel bulb, finely chopped
½ tsp ground cumin
½ tsp ground cloves
1 tsp ground coriander
pinch of saffron threads
300 ml/10 fl oz fish stock
1 preserved or fresh lemon
900 g/2 lb sea bream, cleaned
salt and pepper

method

1 Preheat the slow cooker, if necessary, or according to the manufacturer's instructions.

2 Heat the oil in a large, heavy-based saucepan. Add the onions, garlic, carrots and fennel and cook over a medium heat, stirring occasionally, for 5 minutes. Stir in all the spices and cook, stirring, for a further 2 minutes. Pour in the stock, season with salt and pepper and bring to the boil.

3 Transfer the mixture to the slow cooker. Cover and cook on low for 6 hours or until the vegetables are tender.

4 Rinse the preserved lemon if using. Discard the fish head if you like. Slice the lemon and place the slices in the fish cavity, then place the fish in the slow cooker. Re-cover and cook on high for 30–45 minutes until the flesh flakes easily.

5 Carefully transfer the fish to a platter and spoon the vegetables around it. Cover and keep warm. Transfer the cooking liquid to a saucepan and boil for a few minutes until reduced. Spoon it over the fish and serve.

vegetable curry

ingredients

serves 4–6

2 tbsp vegetable oil
1 tsp cumin seeds
1 onion, sliced
2 curry leaves
2.5-cm/1-in piece fresh ginger,
    finely chopped
2 fresh red chillies, deseeded
    and chopped
2 tbsp curry paste
2 carrots, sliced
115 g/4 oz mangetout
1 cauliflower, cut into florets
3 tomatoes, peeled and chopped
85 g/3 oz frozen peas, thawed
½ tsp turmeric
150–225 ml/5–8 fl oz hot
    vegetable or chicken stock
salt and pepper

method

1 Preheat the slow cooker, if necessary, or according
   to the manufacturer's instructions.

2 Heat the oil in a large, heavy-based saucepan. Add the
   cumin seeds and cook, stirring constantly, for 1–2
   minutes until they give off their aroma and begin to
   pop. Add the onion and curry leaves and cook, stirring
   occasionally, for 5 minutes until the onion has softened.
   Add the ginger and chillies and cook, stirring
   occasionally, for 1 minute.

3 Stir in the curry paste and cook, stirring, for 2 minutes,
   then add the carrots, mangetout and cauliflower
   florets. Cook for 5 minutes, then add the tomatoes,
   peas and turmeric and season with salt and pepper.
   Cook for 3 minutes, then add 150 ml/5 fl oz of the stock
   and bring to the boil.

4 Transfer the mixture to the slow cooker. If the
   vegetables are not covered, add more hot stock,
   then cover and cook on low for 5 hours until tender.
   Remove and discard the curry leaves before serving.

variation

For a creamier curry, stir in 125 ml/4 fl oz of coconut milk
at the end of cooking and heat through before serving.

vegetable goulash

ingredients

serves 4

15 g/^{1}/$_2$ oz sun-dried
    tomatoes, chopped
2 tbsp olive oil
^{1}/$_2$–1 tsp crushed dried chillies
2–3 garlic cloves, chopped
1 large onion, cut into
    small wedges
1 small celeriac, cut into
    small chunks
225 g/8 oz carrots, sliced
225 g/8 oz new potatoes,
    cut into chunks
1 small acorn squash, peeled,
    deseeded and chopped
2 tbsp tomato purée
300 ml/10 fl oz vegetable stock
225 g/8 oz Puy lentils
1–2 tsp hot paprika
3 fresh thyme sprigs,
    plus extra to garnish
450 g/1 lb tomatoes, chopped
soured cream, to serve

method

1 Preheat the slow cooker, if necessary, or according
   to the manufacturer's instructions.

2 Put the sun-dried tomatoes in a small heatproof bowl,
   add freshly boiled water to cover and leave to soak for
   15–20 minutes.

3 Heat the oil in a heavy-based saucepan. Add the
   chillies, garlic, onion, celeriac, carrots, potatoes and
   squash and cook over a medium–low heat, stirring
   frequently, for 5–8 minutes until softened. Mix together
   the tomato purée and stock in a jug and stir it into the
   pan. Add the lentils, sun-dried tomatoes with their
   soaking liquid, the paprika and thyme and bring to
   the boil.

4 Transfer the mixture to the slow cooker, cover and cook
   on low for 4^1/$_2$ hours. Add the tomatoes, re-cover and
   cook on high for 45 minutes until all the vegetables
   and lentils are tender. Remove and discard the thyme
   sprigs. Serve the goulash topped with soured cream
   and garnished with extra thyme sprigs.

moroccan vegetables

ingredients

serves 4

4 tomatoes, peeled,
    deseeded and chopped
700 ml/1¼ pints vegetable stock
1 onion, sliced
2 carrots, diagonally sliced
1 tbsp chopped fresh coriander
175 g/6 oz courgettes, sliced
1 small turnip, cubed
425 g/15 oz canned chickpeas,
    drained and rinsed
½ tsp ground turmeric
¼ tsp ground ginger
¼ tsp ground cinnamon
225 g/8 oz couscous
salt
fresh coriander sprigs, to garnish

method

1 Preheat the slow cooker, if necessary, or according to the manufacturer's instructions.

2 Put half the tomatoes in a blender or food processor and process until smooth. Scrape into a saucepan, add 450 ml/16 fl oz of the stock and bring to the boil. Pour the mixture into the slow cooker, add the remaining tomatoes, the onion, carrots, coriander, courgettes, turnip, chickpeas, turmeric, ginger and cinnamon and stir well. Cover and cook on high for 3 hours.

3 Just before serving, bring the remaining stock to the boil in a large pan. Add a pinch of salt and sprinkle in the couscous, stirring constantly. Remove the pan from the heat, cover and leave to stand for 5 minutes.

4 Fluff up the grains of couscous with a fork and divide it between 4 bowls. Top with the vegetable stew, garnish with coriander sprigs and serve.

sweet & sour sicilian pasta

ingredients

serves 4

4 tbsp olive oil

1 large red onion, sliced

2 garlic cloves, finely chopped

2 red peppers, deseeded and sliced

2 courgettes, cut into batons

1 aubergine, cut into batons

450 ml/16 fl oz passata

4 tbsp lemon juice

2 tbsp balsamic vinegar

55 g/2 oz stoned black olives, sliced

1 tbsp sugar

400 g/14 oz dried fettucine or pappardelle

salt and pepper

fresh flat-leaf parsley sprigs, to garnish

method

1 Preheat the slow cooker, if necessary, or according to the manufacturer's instructions.

2 Heat the oil in a large, heavy-based saucepan. Add the onion, garlic and peppers and cook over a low heat, stirring occasionally, for 5 minutes. Add the courgettes and aubergine and cook, stirring occasionally, for 5 minutes more. Stir in the passata and 150 ml/5 fl oz water and bring to the boil. Stir in the lemon juice, vinegar, olives and sugar and season with salt and pepper.

3 Transfer the mixture to the slow cooker. Cover and cook on low for 5 hours until all the vegetables are tender.

4 To cook the pasta, bring a large saucepan of lightly salted water to the boil. Add the pasta and bring back to the boil. Cook for 10–12 minutes until the pasta is tender but still firm to the bite. Drain and transfer to a warmed serving dish. Spoon the vegetable mixture over the pasta, toss lightly, garnish with parsley and serve.

desserts

chocolate pots

ingredients

serves 6

300 ml/10 fl oz single cream
300 ml/10 fl oz milk
225 g/8 oz plain chocolate,
    broken into small pieces
1 large egg
4 egg yolks
4 tbsp caster sugar
150 ml/5 fl oz double cream
grated chocolate, to decorate

method

1 Preheat the slow cooker, if necessary, or according to the manufacturer's instructions.

2 Pour the single cream and milk into a saucepan and add the chocolate. Set the pan over a very low heat and stir until the chocolate has melted and the mixture is smooth. Remove from the heat and leave to cool for 10 minutes.

3 Beat together the egg, egg yolks and sugar in a bowl until combined. Gradually stir in the chocolate mixture until thoroughly blended, then strain into a jug.

4 Divide the mixture between 6 ramekins and cover with foil. Stand the ramekins on a trivet in the slow cooker and pour in enough boiling water to come about halfway up the sides of the ramekins. Cover and cook on low for 3–3½ hours, until just set. Remove the slow cooker pot from the base and leave to cool completely. Remove the ramekins and chill in the refrigerator for at least 4 hours.

5 Whip the double cream in a bowl until it holds soft peaks. Top each chocolate pot with a little of the whipped cream and decorate with grated chocolate. Serve immediately.

chocolate & walnut sponge

ingredients

serves 4

55 g/2 oz cocoa powder,
    plus extra for dusting
2 tbsp milk
115 g/4 oz self-raising flour
pinch of salt
115 g/4 oz unsalted butter,
    softened, plus extra for
    greasing
115 g/4 oz caster sugar
2 eggs, lightly beaten
55 g/2 oz walnut halves, chopped
whipped cream, to serve

method

1 Preheat the slow cooker, if necessary, or according
   to the manufacturer's instructions.

2 Grease a 1.2-litre/2-pint pudding basin with butter.
   Cut out a double round of greaseproof paper that is
   7 cm/2¾ inches wider than the rim of the basin. Grease
   one side with butter and make a pleat in the centre.

3 Mix the cocoa and the milk to a paste in a small bowl.
   Sift together the flour and salt into a separate small
   bowl. Set aside.

4 Beat together the butter and sugar in a large bowl
   until pale and fluffy. Gradually beat in the eggs, a little
   at a time, then gently fold in the sifted flour mixture,
   followed by the cocoa mixture and the walnuts.

5 Spoon the mixture into the prepared basin. Cover the
   basin with the greaseproof paper rounds, buttered-side
   down, and tie in place with string. Stand the basin on
   a trivet in the slow cooker and pour in enough boiling
   water to come about halfway up the side of the basin.
   Cover and cook on high for 3–3½ hours.

6 Remove the basin from the slow cooker and discard
   the greaseproof paper. Run a knife around the inside
   of the basin, then turn out onto a warmed serving dish.
   Serve with whipped cream, dusted with cocoa.

magic lemon sponge

ingredients

serves 4

140 g/5 oz caster sugar
3 eggs, separated
300 ml/10 fl oz milk
3 tbsp self-raising flour, sifted
150 ml/5 fl oz freshly squeezed
    lemon juice
icing sugar, for dusting

method

1 Preheat the slow cooker, if necessary, or according to the manufacturer's instructions.

2 Beat the sugar with the egg yolks in a bowl, using an electric mixer. Gradually beat in the milk, followed by the flour and the lemon juice.

3 Whisk the egg whites in a separate, grease-free bowl until stiff. Fold half the whites into the yolk mixture using a rubber or plastic spatula in a figure-of-eight movement, then fold in the remainder. Try not to knock out the air.

4 Pour the mixture into an ovenproof dish, cover with foil and place in the slow cooker. Add sufficient boiling water to come about one-third of the way up the side of the dish. Cover and cook on high for 2½ hours until the mixture has set and the sauce and sponge have separated.

5 Lift the dish out of the cooker and discard the foil. Lightly sift a little icing sugar over the top and serve.

italian bread pudding

ingredients

serves 6

unsalted butter, for greasing
6 slices panettone
3 tbsp Marsala
300 ml/10 fl oz milk
300 ml/10 fl oz single cream
100 g/3½ oz caster sugar
grated rind of ½ lemon
pinch of ground cinnamon
3 large eggs, lightly beaten

method

1 Preheat the slow cooker, if necessary, or according to the manufacturer's instructions.

2 Grease a pudding basin and set aside. Place the panettone on a deep plate and sprinkle with the Marsala wine.

3 Pour the milk and cream into a saucepan and add the sugar, lemon rind and cinnamon. Gradually bring to the boil over a low heat, stirring until the sugar has dissolved. Remove the pan from the heat and leave to cool slightly, then pour the mixture onto the eggs, beating constantly.

4 Place the panettone in the prepared dish, pour in the egg mixture and cover with foil. Place in the slow cooker and add enough boiling water to come about one-third of the way up the side of the dish. Cover and cook on high for 2½ hours until set.

5 Remove the dish from the slow cooker and discard the foil. Leave to cool, then chill in the refrigerator until required. Loosen the sides of the pudding and turn out onto a serving dish.

rice pudding

ingredients

serves 4

140 g/5 oz short-grain rice
1 litre/1¾ pints milk
115 g/4 oz sugar
1 tsp vanilla extract
ground cinnamon and 4 cinnamon
    sticks, to decorate

method

1 Preheat the slow cooker, if necessary, or according to the manufacturer's instructions.

2 Rinse the rice well under cold running water and drain thoroughly. Pour the milk into a large, heavy-based saucepan, add the sugar and bring to the boil, stirring constantly. Sprinkle in the rice, stir well and simmer gently for 10–15 minutes. Transfer the mixture to an ovenproof dish and cover with foil.

3 Place the dish in the slow cooker and add boiling water to come about one-third of the way up the side. Cover and cook on high for 2 hours.

4 Remove the dish from the slow cooker and discard the foil. Stir the vanilla extract into the rice, then spoon it into heatproof glasses or bowls. Dust lightly with ground cinnamon and decorate with cinnamon sticks.

variation

For a fruity rice pudding, add 2 tablespoons of crystallized ginger and 2 tablespoons of chopped plumped dried apricots and stir into the pudding before cooking.

thai black rice pudding

ingredients

serves 4

175 g/6 oz black glutinous rice
2 tbsp soft light brown sugar
450 ml/16 fl oz canned
    coconut milk
225 ml/8 fl oz water
3 eggs
2 tbsp caster sugar

method

1 Preheat the slow cooker, if necessary, or according to the manufacturer's instructions.

2 Mix together the rice, brown sugar and half the coconut milk in a saucepan, then stir in the water. Bring to the boil, then reduce the heat and simmer, stirring occasionally, for 15 minutes, until almost all the liquid has been absorbed. Transfer the mixture into individual ovenproof dishes or 1 large dish.

3 Lightly beat the eggs with the remaining coconut milk and the caster sugar. Strain, then pour the mixture over the rice.

4 Cover the dishes with foil. Stand the dish on a trivet in the slow cooker and pour in enough boiling water to come about one third of the way up the sides of the dish. Cover and cook on high for 2–2½ hours, until set. Carefully remove the dishes from the slow cooker and discard the foil. Serve hot or cold.

apple crumble

ingredients

serves 4

55 g/2 oz plain flour
55 g/2 oz rolled oats
150 g/5½ oz light
    muscovado sugar
½ tsp grated nutmeg
½ tsp ground cinnamon
115 g/4 oz butter, softened
4 cooking apples, peeled,
    cored and sliced
4–5 tbsp apple juice
single cream or natural yogurt,
    to serve

method

1 Preheat the slow cooker, if necessary, or according
   to the manufacturer's instructions.

2 Sift the flour into a bowl and stir in the oats, sugar,
   nutmeg and cinnamon. Add the butter and mix in
   with a pastry blender or the prongs of a fork.

3 Place the apple slices in the base of the slow cooker
   and add the apple juice. Sprinkle the flour mixture
   evenly over them. Cover and cook on low for 5½ hours.

4 Serve hot, warm or cold, with single cream or yogurt.

blushing pears

ingredients

serves 6

6 small ripe pears
225 ml/8 fl oz ruby port
200 g/7 oz caster sugar
1 tsp finely chopped
    crystallized ginger
2 tbsp lemon juice
whipped cream or Greek yogurt,
    to serve

method

1 Preheat the slow cooker, if necessary, or according to the manufacturer's instructions.

2 Peel the pears, cut them in half lengthways and scoop out the cores. Place them in the slow cooker.

3 Mix together the port, sugar, ginger and lemon juice in a jug and pour the mixture over the pears. Cover and cook on low for 4 hours until the pears are tender.

4 Leave the pears to cool in the slow cooker, then carefully transfer to a bowl, cover and chill in the refrigerator until required.

5 To serve, partially cut each pear half into about 6 slices lengthways, leaving the fruit intact at the stalk end. Carefully lift the pear halves onto serving plates and press gently to fan out the slices. Serve with whipped cream or yogurt.

poached peaches in marsala

ingredients

serves 4–6

150 ml/5 fl oz Marsala
175 ml/6 fl oz water
4 tbsp caster sugar
1 vanilla pod, split lengthways
6 peaches, cut into wedges and
    stoned or 12 apricots,
    halved and stoned
2 tsp cornflour
crème fraîche or Greek yogurt,
    to serve

method

1 Preheat the slow cooker, if necessary, or according
  to the manufacturer's instructions.

2 Pour the Marsala and 150 ml/5 fl oz of the water into
  a saucepan and add the sugar and vanilla pod. Set
  the pan over a low heat and stir until the sugar has
  dissolved, then bring to the boil without stirring.
  Remove from the heat.

3 Put the peaches into the slow cooker and pour the
  syrup over them. Cover and cook on high for 1–1½
  hours, until the fruit is tender.

4 Using a slotted spoon, gently transfer the peaches to
  a serving dish. Remove the vanilla pod from the slow
  cooker and scrape the seeds into the syrup with the
  point of a knife. Discard the pod. Stir the cornflour
  to a paste with the remaining water in a small bowl,
  then stir into the syrup. Re-cover and cook on high
  for 15 minutes, stirring occasionally.

5 Spoon the syrup over the fruit and leave to cool
  slightly. Serve warm or chill in the refrigerator for
  2 hours before serving with crème fraîche or yogurt.

crème brûlée

ingredients

serves 6

1 vanilla pod
1 litre/1¾ pints double cream
6 egg yolks
100 g/3½ oz caster sugar
85 g/3 oz soft light brown sugar

method

1 Preheat the slow cooker, if necessary, or according to the manufacturer's instructions.

2 Using a sharp knife, split the vanilla pod in half lengthways, scrape the seeds into a saucepan and add the pod. Pour in the cream and bring just to the boil, stirring constantly. Remove from the heat, cover and leave to infuse for 20 minutes.

3 Whisk together the egg yolks and caster sugar in a bowl until thoroughly mixed. Remove and discard the vanilla pod from the pan, then whisk the cream into the egg yolk mixture. Strain the mixture into a large jug.

4 Divide the mixture between 6 ramekins and cover with foil. Stand the ramekins on a trivet in the slow cooker and pour in enough boiling water to come about halfway up the sides of the ramekins. Cover and cook on low for 3–3½ hours, until just set. Remove the slow cooker pot from the base and leave to cool completely. Remove the ramekins and chill in the refrigerator for at least 4 hours.

5 Preheat the grill. Sprinkle the brown sugar evenly over the surface of each dessert, then cook under the grill for 30–60 seconds, until the sugar has melted and caramelized. Alternatively, you can use a cook's blowtorch. Chill for a further hour before serving.

almond charlotte

ingredients

serves 4

unsalted butter, for greasing
10–12 sponge fingers
300 ml/10 fl oz milk
2 eggs
2 tbsp caster sugar
55 g/2 oz blanched
    almonds, chopped
4–5 drops of almond extract

sherry sauce

1 tbsp caster sugar
3 egg yolks
150 ml/5 fl oz cream sherry

method

1 Preheat the slow cooker, if necessary, or according to the manufacturer's instructions.

2 Grease a 600-ml/1-pint pudding basin with butter. Line the basin with the sponge fingers, cutting them to fit and placing them cut-sides down and sugar-coated sides outwards. Cover the base with some of the offcuts.

3 Pour the milk into a saucepan and bring just to the boil, then remove from the heat. Beat together the eggs and sugar in a heatproof bowl until combined, then stir in the milk. Stir in the almonds and almond extract.

4 Carefully pour the mixture into the prepared basin and cover with foil. Stand the basin on a trivet in the slow cooker and pour in enough boiling water to come about halfway up the side of the dish. Cover and cook on high for 3–3½ hours, until set.

5 To make the sherry sauce, put the sugar, egg yolks and sherry into a heatproof bowl. Set the bowl over a pan of simmering water. Whisk well until the mixture thickens, but do not boil. Remove from the heat.

6 Carefully remove the basin from the slow cooker and discard the foil. Leave to stand for 2–3 minutes, then turn out onto a warmed serving plate. Pour the sherry sauce around it and serve immediately.

index

almond charlotte 206
apple crumble 198
aubergine timbales 32

bacon & lentil soup 20
baked asparagus &
    spinach risotto 132
baked aubergine with
    courgette & tomato 84
barbecue chicken 120
beans
    Boston baked beans 28
    four bean chilli 86
    Greek bean & vegetable
        soup 16
    ham with black-eyed
        beans 66
    mixed bean chilli 136
    tex-mex bean dip 22
    Tuscan beans 134
beef
    beef & button onions 58
    beef bourguinon 168
    Caribbean beef 166
    chunky beef chilli 90
    goulash 62
    Neapolitan beef 164
    pot roast with beer 54
    Provençal beef & olives
        60
    spicy beef 56
    traditional pot roast 92
blushing pears 200
Boston baked beans 28
bouillabaisse 172
brunswick chicken 142
Bulgarian chicken 150

cabbage roulades with
    tomato sauce 34
Caribbean beef 166
carrot & coriander soup 12
chicken
    barbecue chicken 120
    brunswick chicken 142
    Bulgarian chicken 150
    chicken & apple pot 46
    chicken & sweetcorn
        stew 42
    chicken braised with red
        cabbage 44

chicken cacciatore 116
chicken & dumplings
    40
chicken Italian-style 148
chicken noodle soup 8
chicken in riesling 118
chipotle chicken 144
cock-a-leekie soup 18
easy Chinese chicken
    152
Florida chicken 146
jambalaya 160
nutty chicken 114
Parmesan chicken 38
slow roast chicken 112
sweet & sour chicken
    wings 24
chocolate
    chocolate & walnut
        sponge 188
    chocolate pots 186
chunky beef chilli 90
cinnamon lamb 102
cock-a-leekie soup 18
crème brûlée 204

duckling
    duckling with apples 94
    jambalaya-style duckling
        154

easy Chinese chicken 152

Florida chicken 146
four bean chilli 86
French-style fish 126

goulash 62
    vegetable goulash 178
Greek bean & vegetable
    soup 16

ham with black-eyed
    beans 66

Italian bread pudding 192

jambalaya 160
jambalaya-style duckling
    154

lamb
    cinnamon lamb 102
    lamb with red peppers
        64
    lamb shanks with olives
        100
    lamb tagine 96
    Mediterranean lamb
        with apricots &
        pistachio nuts 170
    springtime lamb with
        asparagus 98
Louisiana courgettes 30

magic lemon sponge 190
maple-glazed pork ribs 110
Mediterranean lamb
    with apricots & pistachio
    nuts 170
Mexican pork chops 156
mixed bean chilli 136
mixed Mediterranean
    shellfish 124
mixed vegetables 138
Moroccan sea bream 174
Moroccan vegetables 180

Neapolitan beef 164
New England clam
    chowder 10
nutty chicken 114

Parmesan chicken 38
pesto turkey pasta bake 52
poached peaches in
    marsala 202
poached salmon with dill
    & lime 130
pollock bake 128
poor man's cassoulet 158
pork
    maple-glazed pork ribs
        110
    Mexican pork chops 156
    Oriental pork 162
    pork & vegetable ragout
        106
    pork with almonds 104
    spicy pulled pork 108
pot roast with beer 54
Provençal beef & olives 60

rice pudding 194
rice pudding, Thai black
    196

seafood in saffron sauce 122
slow roast chicken 112
south-western seafood 72
spiced seafood & okra 70
spicy beef 56
spicy pulled pork 108
spring vegetables 76
springtime lamb with
    asparagus 98
sweet & sour chicken
    wings 24
sweet & sour Sicilian
    pasta 182

tagliatelle
    tagliatelle with prawns
        68
    tagliatelle with tuna 74
tex-mex bean dip 22
Thai black rice pudding
    196
tomato & lentil soup 14
traditional pot roast 92
turkey
    pesto turkey pasta bake
        52
    turkey & rice casserole
        50
    turkey hash 48
Tuscan beans 134

vegetables
    parsley dumplings 78
    vegetables & lentils 82
    vegetable curry 176
    vegetable goulash 178
    vegetable hotpot with
        parsley dumplings 78
warm chickpea salad 26
winter vegetables 80